WELL
WATERED

never thirst

MELISSA IRWIN

See pp. 60–61

ISBN-10: 147911863X
EAN-13: 9781479118632
Library of Congress Control Number: 2012916444
CreateSpace Independent Publishing Platform
North Charleston, South Carolina

Dedicated to my patient, loving and supportive husband, Joe. Jesus has taught me a lot through you. Also to my three sons whom I love beyond words to describe. Spencer, Asher and Shawn, you are my greatest blessings. Finally, to every orphan or vulnerable child I have had the gift to serve through Beautiful Feet Global Outreach, Inc., you have blessed my life with every expression of your hope.

Special thank yous to every woman I have ever had the pleasure to join in Bible study. You have challenged me and helped me to grow in ways I never fathomed. I love you all and overflow with thankfulness for your moments and investments into my life. To my mom with gratitude for always believing in me. Finally, thank you to Michelle Jeffcoat and Tracy Benner for your golden contributions to the first draft of this book. Your grace and love have made my heart richer.

PREFACE

Since the days that I finally got over myself, I have graciously walked a rewarding journey with Jesus. No longer a slave to my former ways or an outcast in my own mind, I dipped my toes into His stream of living water and mercifully He accepted me. Jesus is just like that, accepting of all who follow His loving lead. But I'll be honest, sometimes I fail to follow, and there are times when I wake up in my life and wonder how exactly I got off track. When I seek Him again and again, He reminds me that He is always going to be there and His path is always for me.

I know that I am not alone in this struggle between staying on His path to righteousness and detouring through the world. This book is my awakening from Him through precious revelations that He has brought to life in my heart. I share these pages with you because I love Jesus and believe that He has asked me to express, through my faith journey, the mysteries He has revealed that have taught me He is accessible. His path has room for you, His stream is abundant, and He is awaiting the dipping in of your toes.

So who I am, this Melissa Irwin of whom you've never before heard? That's not so difficult for me to answer. I'm a formerly twisted, tangled, battered, and broken soul who has trusted in Christ to smooth me out bit by bit over the past twelve years, since my Christian journey began. While not yet wrinkle-free, I'm a servant with a pen responding to the calling to write it out from one end to the other—these mysteries and whispers of hope—so that you too might seek Him for your soul straightening.

"When peoples care for you and cry for you, they can straighten out your soul."

Langston Hughes

One of my sweet friends posted this quote on her Facebook page recently, and when I read it I came undone. Don't we each, from time to time, need a little soul straightening? I can sure confess that I do. My soul needs straightening because it gets twisted up and tangled in knots. It needs to be straightened because life causes it to bend, shrink, swell, and break. This is just my wild imagination talking here; I feel from my heart, but the soul is where I believe and exist. Hope, faith, and love travel back and forth from heart to mind and somehow link the two. The soul is the very core that has been carved and pressed, soldered and sewn. Without a soul, there is no heart. When a soul is damaged, nothing works properly. Cares and cries from the hearts of others are like two gentle hands, smoothing you down from one end to the other, a healing, holy touch.

Oh, Lord, with Your guidance and heart, I want to be a soul straightener. I want to extend my care and increase my cry. I want to bend and kneel and wail and sob on behalf of gnarly souls. This is life, Lord, fragile like bare feet walking on shards of shattered world. And please almighty Savior, show me who my soul straighteners are...the ones You've sent to smooth me out. Show us all who You've sent in Your name into our lives who with Your hands can help us smooth out our wrinkles, from one end to the other. In Jesus, amen

TABLE OF CONTENTS

INTRODUCTION

Throughout the Bible, imagery is used to paint a clear, visual exhibit for us of the relationship Christ invites His followers to join in and actively participate in.

We are thirsty, but He is living water.
Jesus is the vine, and we are branches.
We are seed planters, but God makes them grow.
He is the light and we are lampstands.

Well Watered is intended to be a journey through these various imageries onward toward the destination of knowing Christ better, and then dwelling with Him eternally.

Christ, my never failing King, guide me. I am neither author nor inventor, neither wordsmith nor poet. I am your little girl, and because of You, I am filled with hope in my soul, and my heart is swelled with love I didn't know before You rescued me. May these pages belong to You. May they be true. May they inspire hope in others, hope that increases the knowledge of Your presence and hope that inspires Your Spirit to pull up a throne in the hearts of many, stake claim, and reside forever. Thank you, Jesus, for the courage to share my love for You. In glory, amen.

PART I

~ His Well ~

But where shall we dwell?

I've heard that a life lived for Him should be centered at the well.

THE CHUNKY BITS

So, here we go—the meat of this thing. Before I dive into the chewy part of this chunky stew He has concocted with me, I have been called to share some of the specific ingredients that make up my story. It frightens me at my core to expose my past sin and my present sin, because I do not want to be judged by you. I would prefer that you like me. I do not want to be discarded by my friends and family. I do not want to disappoint my husband, and I do not want to lose the love of my children. But greater than my wants involving my reputation and deeper than my desire to spare my loved ones from hurt is my commitment to serve the One who loved me through it all, washed me clean, and made me new. Despite it all, by His Spirit I am convinced that the end of my story is glory.

Prior to my surrendered life in 1999, I was involved in significant sexual promiscuity, envy, malice, abortion, deception, abuse of trust, financial destruction, and deep, bitter hatred. No one has sought control more vehemently than I have. I lived through two divorces and eleven years of single parenthood. So if you need to know whether I have experienced darkness, I have. If you need to know if I know suffering, I do.

I have been abandoned, neglected, and left to figure out survival. I have been betrayed, discarded, suffered tragic loss and have attempted suicide. I have been let go of and walked away from. I have been buried and broken by the weight of hefty loads of baggage. And these days I still face temptations to lust, to envy, and to shoot cheap-shot arrows into the hearts of people I find difficult to like. I still battle with control issues, fear, worry, and the earthly attraction to "stuff."

So, am I an expert on grace and mercy? Sure, I'm swimming in it. Do I know about redemption and restoration? I absolutely do, because I'm not who I once was. I'm a humbled receiver of the most beautiful gift known to fallen man. And the following chapters are revelations of the mysteries and wisdom He has shown me. They are an effort to piece together the how and the why. Through dirt, flowers, birds, water, children, songs, struggles, and relationships, the Lord of all creation has given me tools to love, to serve, and to mature in faith. He has placed the conviction in my heart to share these tools with you.

My gift to you is from Him too: it is the gift of encouragement. It is the whisper that says, "Keep going. Don't stop short of the blessings God has in store for you."

So, here we go.

CHAPTER I

ON THE PATH

PLAYGROUND

My children crack me up. They stretch me, flex me, and completely wind me up. I can barely whisper the word *playground* and they rejoice with all their energy. Off we go to a local playground, and vocal volumes hit high pitch as I look for a parking space. A minor stampede ensues as they get out of the vehicle and enter chaotic bliss: they climb, swing, slide, spin, hang, jump, and run freely.

So far our playground escapades have been good and fun. Simple and safe. But I can see my elementary school playground in my mind's eye like it was yesterday, where I played from kindergarten until sixth grade. There were many fun times with treasured playmates, but the problem with recess is that the bullies get to come outside and play too. Boys are known for playing too rough, while girls have their own special methods of stirring up trouble. And what about those playground apparatuses? Seriously, can metal poles really be a good idea?

Sure, in the early years there was fun and excitement, but over time, things seemed to unravel. Or rather, I did. I can hear the sound of bouncy rubber kickballs hitting the black top. And if I close my eyes tightly, I can recall the feeling of the ball rocketing into the back of my head, slamming me face first into the center of a hopscotch square—the taste of the blood and asphalt filling my mouth and the wisp of cool air brushing across the backs of my thighs where my dress no longer shielded my ruffled undies.

I remember hanging with clenched tight fists from the highest monkey bar while I tried to ascertain the softest place to land, only to twist my ankle anyway. There are also vivid memories of losing my balance and becoming disoriented from twisting the chains of my swing around as tight as possible, then leaning backward to unwind like a fiercely spun tornado. I remember the feeling of getting jerked around on the seesaw and vomiting off the edge of the merry-go-round. One time I flew out of my swing and landed on my back, gasping for the wind that had been knocked out of me.

At the pinnacle of those early playground years were the pain and shame of the days that I spent as the star attraction of the I Hate Missy Club. Yep. Good times. *Painful memories. Startling realities.*

The playground. It isn't all fun and games, because one way or another at some point everyone ends up getting hurt. We enter with innocence, believing simply that life is safe and enjoyable. But soon we find ourselves disoriented, seeking safety and a soft place to land, hoping to dodge the unexpected things thrown our direction. And occasionally we eat asphalt. If we are really unfortunate, our undies are exposed at the worst times and in the most crowded locations. I would rather eat asphalt personally, but in life we do not get to choose our playground catastrophe, or series thereof.

Life is hard. It is a serious journey of steep climbs and slippery slides. It is a challenging experiment in finding the most fitting play group and learning how to play fair. For most of us, this effort involves everything from giggles and secret whispers to sucker punches from bullies and accidental tumbles from the highest point of the monkey bars. In life, we all fall. *We are fallen.* And in each of us something breaks. *We are broken.* Eventually, we all need a healer.

These days, my kiddos still think that the playground is like heaven. The bully hasn't shown up for them yet. They have not yet eaten asphalt or been hurled into the air by a defective swing. Their time to face recess dangers will come, and when it does, they will gradually understand that this playground is rough. Once they figure out what heaven is not, perhaps their curiosities will drive them to explore what heaven is: an eternal dwelling place with God to be populated with His authentic believers. I will not teach them that heaven is for good people, but for forgiven people, and that this principle applies to every person who dares to believe, even the bullies and the sucker punchers, the dirt eaters and the undies flashers; the gossips, the cheaters, and the lukewarm bystanders.

Heaven is for the fallen and the broken. When my children understand this, they will have the same calling that we all have as Christians. Please understand that we are not serving the kingdom of God if we are just going through motions, playing nice, and waiting for that "someday" when we will be reunited with lost loved ones in heaven. We are serving the kingdom of heaven only if we are living to increase the population of men, women, and children of God. Belief in Jesus requires genuine faith. Genuine faith inspires action. Action involves love, mercy, kindness, forgiveness, compassion, and every beautiful characteristic of Christ. These actions displayed in the will of God change the world. They increase the population of heaven, our eternal playground.

There is not a single nasty playground antic that God refuses to forgive, and there is no level of brokenness that He cannot restore. We need to know this for ourselves, but we also need to know this for our enemies and our opposition. The gospel of Christ is meant for every ear. The hope of heaven is designed for every heart. If you belong to Him, you are a disciple, a co-missioner, an agent, a representative, and an ambassador. He has called us to be bright and to be bold, to zoom out, not in.

These pages are intended to be an exploration of and an encouragement in how we can grow in His love and serve the kingdom of heaven for His glory. My prayer is that we will abandon the lives that we currently lead—attempting just to survive the earthly playground—and live lives that point to and move toward heaven, with our hands holding those of everyone we can reach.

Illume

There is much that perplexes me in this faith journey. So much that I spend a lot of time pondering the depths of a relationship with Christ and searching for answers that I'm certain have been spelled out countless times by those who have gone before me. Many amazing men and women of God have already documented their spiritual aha moments, which are gifts of hope that I believe God uses to deliver sparkles of light into dark places. I thank Him endlessly for the transformed lives He has shaped in this world who are willing to reveal the dark places where they once hid. Some have been genuine, boldly authentic, and hopelessly transparent. He has shone on them, in them, and through them to reveal His readiness to forgive and His delight in redeeming and restoring.

At the very core of me, I believe that the darker we've lived, the more brightly we can shine. For this reason, I sometimes find myself feeling a bit of sorrow for those who haven't ever found themselves face down in a slimy pit. Think about it this way: when we see a news headline about a family who has been rescued from a car that drove off the road into a ravine, we breathe a sigh of relief. What a feel-good story! But when we see headlines about children rescued after four days underneath the rubble left by an earthquake, we are brought to tears and shouts of joy. Why? Because their rescue was highly unlikely. Their salvation, against all odds, was miraculous.

So, if you have been rescued or are in the process of being rescued from a stronghold of addiction, promiscuity, crime, or other disappointing behaviors, you can rejoice in this truth: the darker you have lived, the more brilliantly bright an impact you can have on the hurting world around you. Those still dwelling in the same pits you once dwelt in will recognize your former prison and desire your present freedom.

Everyone has a ministry. Yes, you. Jesus chose you. And why wouldn't He? You have a story to tell because you have been miraculously transformed. Someone in your midst will see the light within you and will see hope for himself or herself. The story of your redemption is not to be hidden and wasted, or to be silently appreciated. The end of your story is glory. You were not redeemed and restored solely for your own benefit. You are a lampstand shining His light on the paths of others. You are a container of the Lord's light. *You* contain *Him*. Shine.

Sometimes I wonder how many of us realize that we were put on this earth to do more than live. We, as Christians, were put here to shine. Bright. Not everyone shines. In fact, many usher in darkness. If you believe that Christ Jesus is the Son of God, the Savior of the world, you must also believe that He has commanded you to shine. He has made it possible for you to expose His very Spirit to the world, and He is ever working to transform the darkness of your sin into a glow that reveals who He is. Like a string of lights on a Christmas tree intended for beauty when all the other lights have gone out, together we enlighten the way. We actively show the world who He is. This is what He has called us to.

We make this complicated. But He made it simple. Jesus taught his disciples that the greatest command is love. Love God. Love others. We are taught poignantly in 2 John 1:6 what love is: "And this is love; that we walk in obedience to his commands. As you have heard from the beginning, his command is that you walk in love." Scripture teaches us that Jesus is the light of the world and that His Word is a lamp unto our feet and a light unto our path. In other words, His word in Scripture shows us the way. When we turn our hearts to this highest priority—that is, to walk in love—we become the glow that illumes the paths for the feet of others. Not because we have a brightness on our own, but because He is within us and He alone lights us up to become radiant beams that illuminate the path into eternity. John 8:12 tells us that Jesus said, "I am the light of this world. Whoever follows me will never walk in darkness, but will have the light of life." To follow Him is to have the light of life. A light that others bear witness to. His light in us does more than improve visibility. It edifies.

This is not meant to come off as poetry. This is a command that many of us do not take seriously enough. It is not merely suggested in Scripture that we have a light within us and that if we could possibly find some time, we could maybe flick it on once in a while in the hopes that someone's way might be made a little easier. We are called to share the beautiful pieces of Him that He brings alive in us, because this is how others find their way to Him.

This is *one* way He gets people's attention. It is also up to us to show mercy, grace, forgiveness, service, compassion, gentleness, kindness, patience, faith, self-control, and love. Not just the easy love— we are to display love that doesn't even make sense. Love to the enemy, the betrayer, the abuser, the gambler, the porn addict, the sexually impure, the wayward brother, the backstabber, and on and on and on and on. This love doesn't make sense. A love that gently rebukes and encourages but also admits when we are wrong. Rarely was Jesus warm and fuzzy in His teachings on love. If anything, He taught us that love is complicated, often painful, and often requires sacrifice. For Him, love suffered the ultimate sacrifice.

If I do not share His love with others in this world, I am guilty of holding His love hostage or not really knowing His love at all. To expose Him, we must know Him. To know Him, we have to seek Him. To seek Him, we must pray, study His Word, and fellowship with other Christians. When we commit our lives to seeking Him humbly and earnestly because we need Him and want Him, He enlarges our hearts' capacity. With that capacity, He equips our hearts to enlarge the kingdom of heaven. If we love Him, we love the flock of sheep He shepherds, and we must desire to reach and to serve the scatterings of the lost.

If we are honest, most of us feel unworthy and ill-equipped to help to enlarge the kingdom of heaven. We look back into the darkness of ourselves and question whether we even belong at all. If we do not question the grace of our own salvation, maybe we toss up excuses as to why we cannot or do not go out into the world and shine for Him: We are shy. We are not knowledgeable enough. We may turn off our friends and loved ones with too much religious speak. We may offend others. Every single one of us comes up with excuses as to why we do not shine, but not one of them is good enough to exempt us from our call. The time is always *now.* People near you are in the dark, and whether or not they know it, they need a little glow to illuminate the path for their next step. Jesus has equipped us to shine, to point to His grace and mercy. May you be encouraged to be a flicker of hope in a world that is covered by a shroud of despair.

JOURNAL ENTRY

~ From the Wet Carpet ~

Even as I close my eyes today, I can float above myself as I lie on the floor, in an almost out-of-body experience.

She was the broken me. Depleted. Horrified. And she was lying in a puddle of her heaviest tears. Her face was wet. Tears pooled up in the creases of her neck and the corners of her mouth. They say you can drown in no more than an inch of water. I say you can drown in your own tears. And she would say that she tried.

I try not to linger here above myself for long, because it burns like a fresh wound. I see her wishing she were dead—and how thankful, overwhelmed, and amazed am I that she is not. Praise Jesus. Only Jesus.

That pool of tears nearly drowning out the existence of her breath led her here to me, where I am now, basking in the light of the One who came to save.

As dreary and as hopeless as those moments were, they were the pinpoints on my lifeline where I cried out to the Lord in one true gesture, a roaring desperate wail. I had been skeptically speaking to Him for years. But this time He recognized the depth of my despair. He knew my lowest point was there on my tear-stained living-room floor. He knew this time I would come without doubt. He knew my white-knuckled grip would not loosen, though the white would slowly fade. He knew this was it. Melissa would finally lean into Him, stretch outside of her comfort zone, pivot her focus onto His design, and grow

into maturity until His work in her would be complete. His…
to the finish.

Divorce took me to the floor that time. After eight and a half
years of being a single mom to a then nine-year-old, I married.
But after a year, my spouse decided his bond to his hobby was
tied with a tighter rope. His decision to leave was quick and simple. For me it was a death, a failure, and an emptiness I pray never
visits me again. But it cannot and it will not, because every empty
hole in my being was filled when Christ rescued me that day in
the floor. The only emptiness left is the longing for my true home
in the heavenly realm, where no carpets are saturated with gut-
wrenching tears. Till then, there are praises to sing, prayers to
raise, journeys to walk, lives to touch, messages to carry, and hope
to spread.

He said, "Come, follow me." Let us.

His Reflection

Like a coin, emptiness is two sided. When I am empty, I have not only
stopped receiving, but also there is nothing left of me to give. Emptiness
is a double-edged, dull blade. It hurts to be unnoticed, worth little, a
portfolio with no investments. When nothing of rich love and sweetness
rests inside me, in my emptiness, I have nothing to offer. Like a well run
dry, I am neither nourished nor nourishing. I am a black hole. It is a tragedy for a child of God to feel this way. Emptiness boils down to lack of
hope. And lack of hope leads to sin and darkness, often manifesting itself
through crime, addiction, abuse, and other behavioral and dependency
issues.

But God created us to be hopeful creatures. He wants our wells to run deep and our buckets to overflow, to never be empty. He would not will for us to be dry, parched, and hopeless. He has so much grace, mercy, and love to pour out abundantly into our lives. He wants us to be full and gloriously drenched in His living water. Jesus said, "'Whoever believes in me, as the Scripture has said, streams of living water will flow from within him.' (By this he meant the Spirit)" (John 7:38-39a). God does not desire for us to be so empty of Him that we can't pour out His love on all those we could so easily and joyfully sprinkle, spray, or just flat-out dunk. His will for us is to be well watered, drenched in His Spirit. His desire is to fill us with His living water and then to see His own reflection in our eyes, the windows to our soul. As Isaiah prophesied, "The Lord will guide you always; he will satisfy your needs in a sun-scorched land and will strengthen your frame. You will be like a well-watered garden, like a spring whose waters never fail" (Isaiah 58:11).

At a young age I heard about the man that died on the cross. As is necessary with children, He was explained to me in a simple fashion. He was a man made from God, for God, who had committed no sin. He died and paid the price for our sins so that when we die, we can go to heaven if we believe in Him. Jesus! Jesus was the one who hung on a cross even though He didn't have to. He died and rose again.

If I would spend the remainder of my life believing this, I could whoop up a party in heaven on streets of gold, where I would never again hurt or cry. As a child, I believed it. I still do. However, in my aging and maturity in faith, I have come to understand that there are many interpretations of the term *believe*. Some of those interpretations do not define the word in truth. *Belief* is more than a word. It isn't real just because it is spoken. To believe requires more than uttering some syllables. It is more than a wish. It is something that manifests in your heart and mind and soul. Real belief takes over. It transforms.

For twenty-five years I was an untransformed person who said I was a believer. The height of my spiritual experience was to get goose bumps when

Amy Grant sang about Jesus on records. (Yes, records. I am prehistoric). I loved the words she sang, and I wanted it all to be true. I spent a lot of years thinking that I truly believed in Jesus when actually I just wanted to believe. I was wishing for it to be true, which is not the same. It wasn't until I was transformed into a person who accepted, admitted, and was certain of the truth of what I had been told as a child that I realized that there was a difference between being a person who *said* I believed and *actually* believing in the truth of it.

Have you ever been on a boat or stood out on a dock and seen your reflection on the waters? You know that it is your image from the shape or position. It is not a clear reflection of you, as if in a mirror, but you know it is you because you know where you are and you are vaguely recognizable. There may be ripples in the water or a dark haze, but you are able to see yourself. There is opacity and movement, but you can see yourself in the reflection of the water and from the light provided by the sun. The sunnier the day, the more clarity in the view.

In this same way, do we capture a glimpse of the spirit and character of Christ at the end of the day; was He reflected in our thoughts, actions, and words? It depends on how much of the Son was in our day. Are we letting Him into all our dark places? Jesus's presence brings light. He is light, and He reveals Himself to us.

Until your belief is authentic, you will seek your own reflection in rippling waters. Once you are convinced that your heart is linked to His Spirit by grace, you will seek Him in the reflection instead. He will transform you to become more like Him; not only will you look for Him, but you will care more and more about how you are reflecting Him to others out into the world. In the same way that you may have the eyes of your mother or hair like your father's, your spirit will bear a resemblance to Christ. We cannot ever hope to be his identical twin, but any measure of resemblance to Christ is glorious. When capturing a glimpse of ourselves at the end of the day, our resemblance to Him will have been in our words, actions, and thoughts. At that point we can ask ourselves how much we actually resemble Him. And He will gradually reveal Himself to us.

Let's get real for a moment. This side of heaven we will never be able to see Jesus in our reflection with the clarity of a freshly cleaned mirror. But He should be recognizable enough in us that we can reflect Him as if in water. It is possible for us to recognize Him in ourselves, and it is possible for others to see Him when they glance in our direction, when they hear us speak, when they see us love, and when they observe us serving others. Even if they do not know they are seeing Him, they should see something in us that they are drawn to, something that they like and long to possess: the very essence of Him, His Spirit manifested in human hearts.

Before we meet Him face to face, He desires for us to see a bit of Him in our own reflection, a resemblance of His character. As He molds us to perfection in His eyes, He will mold us to love more boldly. As the apostle Paul wrote, "But when perfection comes, the imperfect disappears. When I was a child, I talked like a child, I thought like a child, I reasoned like a child. When I became a man, I put childish ways behind me. Now we see but a poor reflection as in a mirror; then we shall see face to face. Now I know in part; then I shall know fully, even as I am fully known" (I Corinthians 13:10-13, NIV). The Word teaches us about love being the "most excellent way," and how it "never fails," "always perseveres," and is the greatest out of all possible spiritual gifts, greater than faith and hope (I Corinthians 13:1-8). The more willing we are to love, the more our reflection resembles Him and the more we present His image to a watching, listening world.

I dream of being a well-watered woman, drenched in His living waters and overflowing. He has given me the gift of a genuine longing within my heart to dream of well-watered men, women, and children across the planet. People from every nation, tribe and of every tongue who reflect Christ. People from every circumstance who have evidence of His Spirit dwelling in their hearts. He is like living water, and we are His. So it only makes sense that we, His children, would have a thirst for His Word and His ways and that we would offer a drink to any person who crosses our path. That we would be well watered because we have been mercifully poured into. That we would be well watered because we reflect Jesus. That we would be well watered because we believe. That we would be well watered because we have joyfully and graciously poured out an overflow of His love from within us.

I praise Your mighty name, sweet Jesus. Pour out onto us, into us, and all the way through us. Give us everything You've got for us, O Lord. May we be drenched in Your Word and Spirit, Your love and Your very truth. Mercifully fill us up, O Lord, and reward us with Your reflection. May all that we have be for You alone. Yes, Jesus. Amen.

Well

Thirsty people will drink contaminated water to stay alive. My first experience serving in orphanages in Africa exposed me to the reality of this; often the result is unnecessary death. A few children had died from cholera just before my arrival, which they had contracted by drinking contaminated water from an impure source. It was known that the water could kill them, and it was understood that not drinking at all would cause death by hydration. It is hard to say what we might do in that situation. Would we risk death to quench our thirst? Or might we risk dehydration in hope that a pure water source might be available before it's too late?

I have seen a bone-dry well. I have also seen a rope tied to a bucket lowered into depth and darkness to rise again with crystal-clear, life-giving refreshment. Empty buckets. Full buckets. Shallow wells. Deep wells. Life giving. Death searching. Abundance. Emptiness.

In certain parts of the world, all hope is centered at the well. All hope. Without a plentiful well, a family may not drink, eat, bathe, work, provide, or survive. The well is the life source.

We with faucets and filled toilet bowls cannot fathom our lives being centered at a well. Due to the advances in technology and modern amenities in our American culture, we may have never gone a day without free-flowing water. We don't even acknowledge the water in our pet's bowl as a luxury. For us water is cheap, available, and purified. Fresh water is lined up in rows by the gallon on shelves in grocery markets, for goodness sake. We may never stop to recognize how vital clean water is to us. We have life because water has life-giving and life-saving power.

No wonder our Jesus refers to Himself in Scripture as living water. He is powerful and life giving. He isn't merely a drink of water but the very *source* of life. He is the wellspring, and He promises that His supply never runs out and will not cease to nourish the believing heart. He is the well from which we draw that never runs dry. And, sweeter yet, He is the very spring of provision that wells up inside of us when we partake of Him, when we follow. I don't know about you, but I desperately need these analogies, the visual being that I am. Jesus's beloved John recorded Him as saying, "But whoever drinks of the water I shall give him shall never thirst; but the water I shall give him shall become in him a well of water springing up to eternal life" (John 4:14, NASB).

He is a well, and He provides us with our own "well" that springs up. I have become fascinated by the word *well*. The Greek word for well is *pe'ge'* (pronounced pay-gay). In the *Holman Hebrew-Greek Keyword Study Bible* (NASB), I learn that the use of the word *well* in this verse suggests a figurative meaning of "life-giving water." That water is not just giving life for today, as we exist as humans on a planet, but life in the everlasting heavenlies. Jesus desires to sustain us not only for today but for eternity. By trusting Christ with the journey of our lives, He automatically drenches us with life-giving waters and journeys with us toward eternity. He knows our own wells will run dry without Him, and His is an eternal source. I have no doubt about His desire and plan that we should be not only watered, but well watered.

The same word for *well* in John 4:14 is also used in Revelation 7:17, and translates as *springs*: "They shall hunger no more, neither thirst anymore; neither shall the sun beat down on them, nor any heat; for the Lamb in the center of the throne shall be their shepherd and shall guide them to *springs* of the water of life; and God shall wipe every tear from their eyes" (Revelation 7:16-17, emphasis added). The very same word is used here but with a slightly different meaning. In this Scripture, the words *springs* and *well* (*pe'ge'*) mean "emblem of highest enjoyment." We can understand this as Jesus filling our hearts with an endless supply of Him for our highest enjoyment.

No matter what life dishes out, no matter the circumstance or depth of darkness we might experience in the sufferings and trials of our daily grinds, He is the very water of life, our life giver. He is the provision of enjoyment that we can *tap* into. At times we may feel positively flooded, while at others we may feel merely a trickle. The enjoyment is in knowing that He is there and in the glorious anticipation of what is to come.

We can glean yet another nugget of beauty here if we are willing to dip deeper into this well. The same word for *well* and *spring* (*pe'ge'*) that we have already explored is also used in Scripture as *flow* and *hemorrhage* in Luke 8:43-44. These verses depict a woman who had been suffering many years of bleeding: "And a woman who had a hemorrhage for twelve years, and could not be healed by anyone, came up behind Him, and touched the fringe of His cloak; and immediately her hemorrhage stopped" (NASB). Like the bleeding woman who reached out for the cloak of Jesus in a desperate search for healing of her twelve long years of bleeding, we can reach out to Him for the healing of our own hemorrhage. Christ hemorrhaged on the cross, paying for our sins so that He could stop the hemorrhage in us and replace the flow with living waters, His very Spirit. With Him, we won't be left unattended to bleed out until lifeless, because He has already bled out on our behalf—offering atonement for our sins. His death resurrected a new covenant, a new life not only for Him but for us as well. Let us be well watered.

Sweet Jesus, in Your mighty name I pray that You will remind us that our daily portion is found in Your well of living waters. That You are more than enough. That no matter what our lives present to us every day, You are the emblem of highest enjoyment. My prayer, Lord, is that Your precious Spirit prompts us daily to tap into You, that we not journey on our own paths but follow Your lead. Please lead us through Scripture, through prayer, through work and service, and through the grace that you pour out like a full bucket from a deep well. Your deep well. In your saving name, amen

CHAPTER 2

NO LONGER POWERLESS

what wells up inside

I continue to go through seasons of exhaustion. Do you? I bet we all do. We all have energy, and we focus it toward something, even if that something is nothing. I know from experience that even doing nothing can be quite exhausting, because when I do nothing, my mind works overtime on self-condemnation. If I could shut off my mind, I could possibly get some rest. I suppose this is why the old saying remains so popular: "There is no rest for the weary."

If Christ is living water and His source forever remains in us, then when we lower our buckets into the depths of His fresh well, it should always come back to us with something in it. His Spirit. Oh, that is such good news to me! *Yes, Lord—that our inner buckets would be filled to the measure with Your very Spirit.* To be soaked, drenched, saturated, well watered by the streams of living water means to be cleansed in and filled by His very Spirit. His Spirit within us is like buckets of power to be treasured. His power overcomes our exhaustion because with Him there is always a reason to keep going. There is light at the end of every dark tunnel.

We are not doing this life alone once we have committed to doing life with Him and for Him. He will see to it that every good thing He has begun will be complete. The apostle Paul said, "Let us not become weary in doing good, for at the proper time we will reap a harvest if we do not give up" (Galatians 6:9). He spoke this over the Roman province of Galatia. It served to encourage the Galatians, and it serves to encourage us still today. Our harvest is ahead. It is bountiful. It is divine. Go in Him.

When Jesus walked on this earth, He was a living man with flesh. Other men and women saw Him, spoke with Him, and touched Him. They encountered His great power firsthand. Yet he wore simple garments. He had hands and feet, knees and elbows, fingers and palms. His friends and followers loved him. So when Jesus began to tell his friends that he would be departing the world soon, of course they were upset. It was sad and frightening to think of the very being of Christ no longer with them. Oh, how it pierces my heart to think of the most treasured loves of my life no longer being here. When our loved ones depart this earth and leave us behind, there is a heavy, painful sense of finality, of permanent separation. We can't stand the thought of this. It is no wonder that we may expend countless tears and countless hours begging in prayer against the very idea of permanent disconnection from the souls we cherish. It's the last thing we want—bidding farewell to our loved ones.

Jesus told his disciples that He would be leaving this world. They had already accepted and believed him to be the Son of God, the Christ Messiah, the very Savior of the world. Now that they had Him, they certainly did not want to lose Him. It didn't make sense. Why would He go? What could the purpose of this be? They rebuked Him and begged him to stay. And they couldn't begin to understand how they would continue His ministry without Him. They wanted Him to be *with* them.

This is difficult for us to fathom as well. I was born in 1970, and by that point the very sandals on Jesus's feet were ancient history. How could I be born 1,970 years beyond His Last Supper, yet still be able to do life *with* Him? He isn't here for me to recline against at the supper table. He isn't here in the flesh for me to witness His hands returning sight to the blind. He isn't here to wipe my tears and cannot relieve my fears in person over a cup of coffee. He does not break bread with me or turn my water into wine.

The physical Christ was one man who died over two thousand years ago. But the Spirit of Christ has been sent to dwell in the hearts of every woman and man who has faith to believe that He is the Son of God. Jesus shared many conversations with his disciples, attempting to explain that when He died, it would be for the sins of the world, and that the Father God would send them (and us) another "friend" in His place—His very Spirit. He said,

"And he [God the Father] will give you another counselor to be with you forever—the Spirit of truth. The world cannot accept him, because it neither sees him nor knows him. But you know him, for he lives with you and will be in you. I will not leave you as orphans; I will come to you." (John 14:16-18)

"If anyone loves me, he will obey my teaching. My Father will love him, and we will come to him and make our home with him." (John 14:23)

"But when he, the Spirit of truth, comes, he will guide you into all truth. He will not speak on his own; he will speak only what he hears, and he will tell you what is yet to come. He will bring glory to me by taking from what is mine and making it known to you." (John 16: 13-14)

When Christ paid the price for the sins of the world and ascended into heaven to be seated at the right hand of the throne of God, He did not leave us. He provided us with an abundant, never-ending source of Himself—a stream of living water welling up inside of you and me—in the form of His Holy Spirit. If you believe in Him, He is in you at all times. Forever *with.*

Not only is His Spirit within you, serving as access to God the Father, His Spirit is an actual down payment on what is yet to come. As Paul wrote to the Corinthian church, "Now it is God who makes both us and you stand firm in Christ. He anointed us, set his seal of ownership on us, and put his Spirit in our hearts as a deposit, guaranteeing what is to come" (2 Corinthians 1:21-22).

Paul also went into the city of Ephesus to encourage the believers there that they too could tap into the living waters. He reminded them, "And you also were included in Christ when you heard the word of truth, the gospel of your salvation. Having believed, you were marked in him with a seal, the promised Holy Spirit, who is a deposit guaranteeing our inheritance until the redemption of those who are God's possession—to the praise of his glory" (Ephesians 1:13-15). That message was not only for the Ephesians, but also for every person since then who has accepted Jesus as the Son of God, the Savior of the world.

What do we need more of today? We always need more of Him. This is where I want us to really grasp a truth, one I feel I missed for a long time: when we partake of Him, He issues a double portion of blessing. He desires to bless you directly, but He also desires for any blessing that you receive to bless others. He issues us enough blessing to spare and share. He blesses us with forgiveness and expects us to be forgiving. He blesses us with hope and tells us to share His hope with others. He may at times bless you with food. Share it. He may bless you with money. Be joyfully generous with it.

God is incredibly patient with us and offers opportunity to be redeemed day after day. Do we offer this same patience and opportunity for redemption to those in our lives who need it most? His patience is a double-portion blessing. He does not intend for His blessings to stop at you and me. He serves up a double portion so that His blessing can reach out far and wide. He is the very root of every fruitful vine. We are taught in Galatians 5:22-23 that the fruits of His Holy Spirit are "love, joy, peace, patience, kindness, goodness, faithfulness, gentleness and self-control" and that "against such things there is no law."

Bottom line: we have far more access than we realize. First, we desperately want forgiveness and salvation, which are the original draw to hope in Him. But what if, as the Bible suggests, there is more? We have access to peace, according to Philippians 4:7: "And the peace of God, which transcends all understanding, will guard your hearts and your minds in Christ Jesus." We also have access to joy and peace, according to Romans 15:13: "May the God of hope fill you with all joy and peace as you trust in him, so that you may overflow with hope by the power of his Holy Spirit."

As I continue in my personal relationship with Christ, I've begun to notice the term *power* used repeatedly throughout the New Testament. Sometimes this power is referencing Jesus Himself. Other times, this power is mentioned with reference to the Holy Spirit within us. If the Holy Spirit is in me and the Spirit has power, does that mean this power is mine? Do I have access to power? This is something I really want to understand. Don't you?

Let's go back a few years. Okay, maybe a few decades. As a little girl, I intently watched television programs about seemingly average human beings with extraordinary powers. I couldn't get enough of Wonder Woman, the Bionic Woman, and Charlie's Angels. Because of my early conditioning, I often mistake *power* to mean something I can never achieve. Let's face the truth: I'll not be leaping over tall buildings with the aid of a trampoline, much less from a standing position. Nor am I likely to deflect bullets with a golden bracelet.

These days I no longer attribute power to superheroes. There are humans these days with perceived power. When we think of power today, don't we immediately think of people with highly visible positions, such as politicians, entertainers, or professional athletes? Even if we don't broaden our perspective that widely, we may quickly call to mind the CEO of the company we work for or the friends with affluent ZIP codes or the acquaintances with luxurious habits. The truth is, whether we want to admit it or not, we often equate power with position in life. If we are not one of those who get the high paycheck, the accolades, the title, or the corner office, we might think we have no power at all.

We must restructure this understanding within us. Each one of us has a platform and a voice. This life lived for Christ isn't a popularity contest. Only His popularity matters. The most popular people in society may not be the most popular to the living God. Every little one of us, no matter how tiny to the world, has a full measure of the incomparably great power of God accessible in our hearts by the Spirit. In simpler terms, a true, believing, surrendered Christian is blessed with powers that we may never fully comprehend. And this is what I love, what gets me so excited and so fired up: we all have power through Christ and His Spirit—power that affects lives.

This is where you might begin to question my sanity. I get that. Twelve years ago, if you had told me over a cup of coffee that I could have spiritual power, I probably would have talked about you behind your back and politely declined all future coffee invites. I knew that Jesus was for my salvation. But now I know He is so much more than that (as if that isn't enough): He is my life, and He has power that I can use. You probably still think I'm crazy, and I get that too, but let's consider the apostle Paul. In his letter to the church in Ephesus, he wrote,

> I pray that out of his glorious riches he may strengthen you with *power through his Spirit* in your inner being so that Christ may dwell in your hearts through faith. And I pray that you, being rooted and established in love, *may have power* together with all the saints to grasp how wide and long and high and deep is the love of Christ. And to know this love, that surpasses knowledge, that you may be filled to the measure with all the fullness of Christ. (Ephesians 3:16-19, NIV, emphasis added)

This Scripture alone fills me with an eagerness I cannot describe and a hope that is bursting like fireworks. It inspires me to love, serve, and share. I pray it does for you too.

Let's begin the analysis of these verses by recognizing that God has an abundance of glorious riches, among them being power that He provides to strengthen us (v. 16). But how does He strengthen us with power? Through His Holy Spirit. Where? In our inner being, the deepest part of you and me. Why? So that a place can be made in the deepest part of each heart for Christ to dwell. We only need to exercise a little bit of faith, amounting to no more than the littlest mustard seed. Glory! Do you see this? It all started with an injection of power by God Himself. Then He goes on to root us directly to Himself (v. 17) and then suggests it would take all of us gathered with every saint to begin to grasp the magnitude of the height, width, length, and depth of His love (v. 18).

Even though we cannot fathom it fully or articulate it with absolute accuracy, we have received His power and are filled to the measure (as full as possible) with so much of Christ Jesus that we might actually begin to resemble Him. We need to know that there is *something* to this power. It isn't to be fought over, because it is available for unlimited distribution. It is only essential that we get that there is *something to it*. It is so very worth exploring.

The Hebrew word for power is *dunamis* (pronounced *doo'-nam-is*). It means many things, including force; ability; abundance; a person in whom the power of God is manifested; power imparted from God; and power imparted by the Holy Spirit. We can interpret this receiving of His Spirit as a force—a force within us. This isn't a sci-fi "may the force be with you" kind of power. An authentic spiritual force it is. With Christ in our hearts, we are blessed with the ability to persevere through life, no matter what obstacles compromises our path. His power within us also translates to having an abundance of mercy, love, and compassion poured out on us daily—the grace He freely gives.

Another meaning of *dunamis* (power) is "a great work." When you and I receive Christ, His Spirit takes up residence in our hearts. Among the many gifts the Spirit unlocks for us to access is "a great work." Again, I see a double portion of blessing here. One is that you and I are a great work, a masterpiece crafted by God Himself. Another is that He has designed a great work for us each to carry out. We are not only masterpieces, works of art to be admired. We are also masterpieces like an airplane or a computer, created to perform critical functions and to help make life better for others. God has empowered us to perform a great work in His name. That great work can be as simple as displaying the love and mercy of God in your relationships and your community so that others can know Him too. The only title or position you need in order to accomplish this is "believer."

I have friends in Africa that go outdoors each day to collect water from their wells. They venture out even if it is raining or dirt is blowing or wild animals are nearby. They even go when the well may be dry. Though the well may be hard to get to and though the bucket may come up empty, this never stops them from approaching the well. I must admit, there are days that I will not drive to the store in my heated vehicle to replenish milk and bread if the wind is too chilly. And though I understand that faith is an opportunity for an exquisite journey with Christ, there are countless days that I do not approach the well. I may have Christ on my mind and in my heart, but I fail to whisper His name, offer a prayer of gratitude, intercede for another, or seek Him through the precious pages of His mighty Word. I may not approach the well of His living waters, of prayer, of praise, of power, and every other perfect gift He offers for my bucket and me.

Approaching the well is work. It involves a little movement—some action. I have to go to it and lower my bucket in. I have to seek the living water. Once I seek, He pours out abundantly; in fact, He may provide such a splash that nearby spectators get drenched in the process. In Him, within the depths of all that He has to offer, my bucket never comes up empty. He fills it with fruit of the Spirit. He will fill it with His power—the many powers He offers to us out of the overflow of His glorious riches.

I invite you to grab your buckets and meet me at the well.

CHAPTER 3

BUCKETS FULL

Buckets of Power

POWER TO CONQUER SUFFERING

The first time I noticed the word *power* in Scripture was in the account in the Gospels of the woman who had been bleeding for twelve years (to read this account, go to Mark 5 and Luke 8). She had been seeking treatment from doctors for many years, but she continued to get worse. She had suffered greatly and had run out of money. She had heard Jesus was in town. I imagine she may have heard the commotion of the crowds of people following Him and perhaps thought, like many of us do, *Jesus, my life isn't going too great without You, so I'm going to reach out and see what You are all about.*

The woman joined the crowd, obviously fed up with the suffering, the blood, the years of not knowing, and the depletion of her resources. She moved behind Him in the crowd. And with her heart beating and believing, *If I just touch his clothes, I will be healed* (Mark 5:28), she reached out and touched His cloak. Scripture says that, in that very instant, Jesus realized that power had left His body. In that same instant the woman stopped bleeding. Somehow His power was transferred to her. And Jesus said, "Someone touched me; I know that power has gone out from me" (Luke 8:46).

The woman was empowered by belief. She was empowered by the reach. She was empowered by a brush with His garment. She was empowered by hope in His name alone. Jesus.

The story could end right there, and it would be delicious, but for our sake, there is a second helping. Jesus felt the power go out of Him, and so He stopped to look around. He even asked who had touched His garment, because he was caught up in a large crowd that had gathered all around him in curiosity. Now, He knew who had reached out to him, but sometimes His knowing isn't enough; He wanted *everyone* to know. (There is so much for us to glean in the seemingly insignificant details.) Couldn't He have just kept walking? Sure, but He prompted the newly healed bleeding woman to step forward and profess Her faith and healing. The story tells us she was "trembling with fear" but that she "fell at his feet and told Him the whole truth." And "he said to her, Daughter, your faith has healed you. Go in peace and be freed from your suffering" (Mark 5:33-34).

Get this, and praise Him: we have access to His power that frees us from suffering. And let us broaden our understanding of "suffering." We do not have to be physically sick to be suffering. Suffering occurs in the mind and the heart every day. We suffer worry. We suffer fear. We suffer doubt. We suffer from old hurts, betrayals, and abandonments. We suffer addictions, pain, hardship, and all kinds of trials. Even if we are not physically healed—in other words, *even if He does not stop the bleeding*—His power in us is more than enough to free us from suffering.

The majority of our human suffering takes place in worried minds and broken hearts. Let us lower our buckets and wash out the suffering our hearts and minds hold onto. Let the living waters wash it all away. I don't mean for it to sound as simple or as rapid as a bath, but Scripture is clear that it is God's will for us to persevere, not to remain in a state of suffering: "Blessed is the man who perseveres under trial, because when he has stood the test, he will receive the crown of life that God has promised to those who love him" (James 1:12). It is God's will for us to be redeemed and restored, and this may require periods of discipline. As is written in Hebrews, "Endure hardship as discipline," and "God disciplines us for our good, that we may share in his holiness. No discipline seems pleasant at the time, but painful. Later on, however, it produces a harvest of righteousness and peace for those who have been trained by it" (12:7a; 12:10b-11).

His well has ample provision of His power to conquer your suffering. Prayers for His will are met with His willingness.

> *Precious Lord, You have promised us freedom in Your name. Help us to know and to be grateful for the hardships that shape us, that forever change us and move us toward You. Father, please guide us to Your abundant well for a portion of the freedom that overcomes every pain, regret, and worry. In You we are conquerors. You have never designed that suffering would weigh us down, flatten us out, and defeat us in our tracks. There is no suffering that You cannot overcome. Overcome us, Lord. Jesus, we want to be free in Your precious name. Amen.*

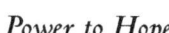

Power to Hope

Have you ever attended a grand buffet—maybe a wedding reception or an appreciation gala—where you stand in a line of happy people eager to fill up a plate with every delicious thing they can set their eyes on? Often you have the opportunity to select your dessert at the time as the main course. I have to admit I love that. I love having a sliver of chocolate staring back at me while I enjoy a large plate of rolls, medium-rare meat, and tossed salad. Well, to tell the truth, I don't wait until the end to enjoy the dessert. I go ahead and take a bite early in my meal, and then another and another. It's just difficult for me to save the best for last when I can enjoy the best all the way through.

I insert this little piece of dessert metaphor to let you know that, as I share what is on my heart in this book about the powers of God, I am not listing them in order. I am not saving the best for last. Like any balanced meal, every portion matters, every calorie counts, and every nutrient is vital. It doesn't matter so much what order they go in, as long as you chew it all up well before you swallow. As I tried to structure the content of these power points, I knew that I had to tell you there are far more powers than I can mention, because I am too human to know it all. I am flawed, so my understanding is limited. My order is random; His order is not. With Him, it's all chocolate! Your greatest and only necessary resource will always be His Word.

Now, let us consider another power of the Spirit that we have access to: the power to hope.

If you think about it, the saddest people in all the earth are the ones who hold not an ounce of hope. It may not seem to fit the equation, but some of the most hope-filled people I have met are those who have nothing else. I believe there may be a correlation between hope and have. It's an inverse relationship: the more we have, the less we hope. The less we have, the more we hope. Hope is the key to going to bed with the desire to wake up tomorrow. Hope keeps us alive, inasmuch as we have any decision in the matter.

The Hebrew word for "hope" is *elpis* (pronounced *el-pece'*). It means simply to anticipate with pleasure, to have a confident expectation of good. The "hope of Christ" specifically refers to eternal life and blessedness. I greatly appreciate the idea that I have the power to wake up each day with a confident expectation of good—to anticipate with pleasure. Each and every morning I have the choice to recognize that His hope is within me, that I have been promised eternal life and blessedness. My day doesn't have to be good or special, and it may go all kinds of wrong. What matters is that I can separate the hope I have in Christ from any hope I might have in my day.

Referring to the Colossians' faith in Jesus and love for the saints, Paul wrote of "the hope laid up for you in heaven of which you previously heard in the word of truth, the gospel" (Colossians 1:5, NASB). I love the succinct nature of the NASB, although I also adore the decoration of the Scripture in the NIV, where the same verse reads like this: "the faith and love that spring from the hope that is stored up for you in heaven and that you have already heard about in the word of truth, the gospel." Paul is teaching the Colossians that the faith they have in Jesus and the love they have for the saints is actually springing from the hope that is stored up in heaven for them.

Does this mean that our hope is in a treasure chest in heaven, and we somehow have access to it today? According to this image painted with words, hope is springing from heaven right into our very being. It springs forth! So perhaps instead of lowering our bucket into a well, wishing for hope, we just hold it up high and receive it from the spring that pours forth from the heavenlies. Either way, buckets of hope contribute to a well-watered soul.

Psalm 9:18 says, "But God will never forget the needy; the hope of the afflicted will never perish" (NIV). No matter what happens today— the circumstances of your life, the darkness of your past or even your present—and no matter your affliction, your hope will never perish. He will always have a full bucket waiting for you. Call out to him. David did in Psalm 31:7-8 (NIV): "I will be glad and rejoice in your love, for you saw my affliction and knew the anguish of my soul. You have not handed me over to the enemy but have set my feet in a spacious place."

No matter what on earth you are facing and no matter how tragic, upsetting, or frightening it is, He knows your affliction, and His hope for you is abundant. It is a treasure, for goodness sake. If you are fresh out of everything, I implore you to go to Him and ask for hope. He may not shape the outcome in your preferred fashion, but He will replenish your hope in Him, in His plan, in His purpose, in His will. Asking for hope is absolutely smack dab in the center of His will, and when His will is prayed with faith and reverence, the answer is "Yes, child." A spring of hope never runs dry.

There are countless examples of hope in Scriptures. One of my favorites is in the book of Genesis, within the story of Abraham. Abraham lived prior to Christ the Messiah, so he did not have the Holy Spirit living in him. He received the word of God directly from the source. God told Abraham some strange things that were very unlikely, so Abraham had to make a decision about whether or not he would believe God. And to be honest, the stuff wasn't very believable. Abraham and his wife, Sarah, were very old and considered to be far beyond childbearing years. They had given up. Hearing from God that Sarah would bear children may have seemed like a sick joke. It surely seemed absurd given her old age.

How many times have we waited and waited for a particular event to take place, only to finally give up? I bet it has happened to each of us at least once. I am forty-one years old and have zero desire to fulfill my childhood dream of being a veterinarian. Zero. It would require far too much work, and I would basically have to start over. I'm getting older, have small children at home, cannot focus the way I used to, and have no inclination toward science. If the Holy Spirit convicted me today that I was to go back to school to become a veterinarian, I would not be pleased. Most likely, I would resist or rebel against it. I might try to deny that I heard the call or felt the prompting. And to think of that possibility now feels incredibly hopeless.

Abraham and Sarah were well into their nineties when God told them they would have children. They had already given up. I love the New Testament reflection back on that event: *"Against all hope,* Abraham, *in hope* believed and so became the father of many nations; just as it had been said to him, 'So shall your offspring be'"* (Romans 4:18, NIV, emphasis added). This blows my mind. Against all hope—in other words, in an utterly hopeless situation. But Abraham hoped anyway. Specifically, "in hope" Abraham chose to believe. Belief required hope. Belief required "a confident expectation of good." He anticipated with pleasure. Abraham believed in eternal life and blessedness. He believed God. His hope was in the Lord God Almighty.

I'll reiterate what we know by now: we cannot travel well through life without at least a small measure of hope. Why would we ever work or marry or raise children or board an airplane or nurture relationships without at least some small hint of hope? The major concern is whether our hope rests in ourselves or some other human or whether it rests in the belief that God is God, that His will is perfect (even when it hurts), and that heaven exists. Don't allow your well of hope in heaven to sit untapped. Ask God to tip over that bucket and pour it out on you. He absolutely will. You have the key to unlock that treasure. Just believe.

Precious Father, may we be impressed to know in our hearts that You created us to hope and for us to know where our hope belongs—in your hands. May we be like Abraham, having hope against all hope to believe in Your power, Your salvation, and Your eternal kingdom. We are on our way, Jesus. We are running, and we are hoping with every heavy step, with every breath and with every new challenge. You are glory. We place all of ourselves into Your will. By Your grace and mercy we live. We hope. We love. Yes, Jesus. Amen!

Power to Display God's Mercy

I heard the word *mercy* at a very young age. It is a very humorous and light-hearted memory that has no place in this book, but I will share it with you anyway. If nothing else, it may offer some insight into my background—lest you think I grew up in a house of saints. My mother is the oldest of eight children, all born and raised in Arkansas. All of my young life, my little family (Mom, Dad, and I) would load up into the car a few times a year and drive to Lake City, Arkansas, to spend time with my grandparents, aunts, uncles, and cousins. Countless numbers of us piled into a small, three-bedroom, *one* bathroom house and spent the weekend.

The all-time favorite pastime of my aunts and uncles was card playing. The only game of choice was, is, and will always be Pitch. You blindly bid with your partner across the table from you and then proceed to win or lose. Pitch games are loud and competitive. In my family, much cheating took place, and crowns made of aluminum foil were fought for to the end.

What does any of this have to do with mercy? I am *so* glad you asked. My uncle Ricky was a sly, cool cat. He cursed the most, smoked the most, drank the most, and quite possibly won the most games of Pitch. He said, "Mercy," at definitive moments during every game. He uttered, "Mercy," when the last drop of beer was gone. He exclaimed, "Mercy!" when he'd been dealt a bad hand. He shouted, "Mercy!," when he'd won. Basically, *mercy* was his word for every occasion. To me, a young and impressionable child, it sounded like a very cool word, only spoken by very cool, winning people. I had no earthly idea what it meant.

Sorry for the whiplash, but I'm about to turn this car around and drive right back to Jesus. At the very beginning of my "real" faith journey in 1999, I needed desperately to know what *mercy* meant, because I was beginning to hear it in church. I had invested in a study Bible, *The Quest*. Its dictionary offered me this definition of *mercy*, and I value it to this day: compassion or kindness shown to someone instead of severity, especially to someone who doesn't deserve it. (Thank you, *Quest*.)

Mercy is more than forgiveness. It is compassion and kindness expressed when termination or punishment or grounding is deserved. It is the offering of perpetual second chances. Our God promises this to us, and He delivers over and over and over and over. But this journey to the well with our empty buckets isn't just about us. No, it is that double portion of blessing again.

As with all of God's blessings, His mercy is meant to be shared. I need a bucket full of mercy drawn from a deep well that I can pour out over others in my life. God so lavishly douses me with undue compassion and kindness. He is forever granting me another chance. I deserve nothing of His love, and yet He promises He will not withhold it from me. But

He wants me to be generous with my extra portion. He wants me to be merciful to my children, my husband, parents, friends, peers, neighbors, and even total strangers—the stranger who cuts me off in traffic or who blocks the entire aisle at the grocery store or who rides my bumper on the interstate. The mercy He pours out on us is a fully glorious but undeserved gift, as will most of our merciful actions be. The power to be merciful is available to us by the Holy Spirit, and we are meant to display it.

Romans 9:14-17 says, "For [God] says to Moses, 'I will have mercy on whom I have mercy, and I will have compassion on whom I have compassion.' It does not, therefore, depend on man's desire or effort, but on God's mercy. For the Scripture says to Pharaoh: 'I raised you up for this very purpose, that I might display my power in you and that my name might be proclaimed in all the earth'" (NIV). This Scripture is referencing an Old Testament text demonstrating that God has mercy and offers it to whomever He chooses. What I *love* about this text is that God is willing to be merciful to an Egyptian pharaoh who had no reverence for God whatsoever (see Exodus 9).

Here's the full story: Pharaoh had a choice to make about how he would react to God's mercy. He could have obeyed God and received the gift of mercy. If so, God would have displayed His own power through Pharaoh's life. If things had gone that way, Pharaoh would have been lifted up, and God's name would have been proclaimed. It would have been a win-win for both Pharaoh and for God. Pharaoh had been asked to have mercy on God's people, the Israelites whom he had enslaved, to grant them freedom from Egypt so that they could journey into the land God had promised them. Pharaoh was offered mercy in exchange for mercy. (Praise you, sweet Lord).

But Pharaoh refused to be merciful and therefore was punished by God in the form of numerous plagues sent to terrorize him and the Egyptians. God sent a plague on the livestock, a plague of boils, of hail, of locusts, of darkness, and even a plague on the first-born. To us reading these accounts in Exodus today, plagues seem extreme, but what we need to contemplate is the terrorization. How often are we aware that our unwillingness to have mercy on those around us ultimately terrorizes our own hearts and spirits?

As humans living in free will, we have human powers. We have the power to lie, manipulate, and persuade. Humans have been scheming their way into high-powered positions of authority since the beginning of time. The garden of Eden was the first-ever power struggle. Humans wanted to have the same level of knowledge as God. Satan tempted them with that and ultimately deceived them. He dangled the apple offering this knowledge, and they bit. Earthly power is self-centered and almost always becomes a massive monument that crumbles under the weight and pressure. The power of God rests in us through the Holy Spirit, which never crumbles and is none too heavy.

What I am hoping we glean from this portrait of mercy is that *mercy* is a power of God that He wants to display in us. Mercy may be the most difficult to choose and yet the most rewarding attribute of God that He shares with us through Christ and His Holy Spirit. Think about it. Is there anything more difficult than offering kindness, compassion, and forgiveness to someone who has done nothing at all to deserve it? In our lives there are abusers, manipulators, liars, thieves, haters, frauds, vicious attackers, killers, betrayers, accusers, and other evildoers. Good Lord! *Good Lord?* How do we offer mercy to these?

Only by His power are we equipped to be merciful to any of these. There is nothing decent enough or good enough in our inner being that can empower us to offer such a gift on our own. Because of this, there is no better way, time, or place for God to display His power through us than when we do just exactly that: offer mercy to the undeserving.

This is the power that has convinced me over and over that God is real. I have relied on God's power in me to give me the ability to offer kindness and compassion to those who may not deserve it from me. In doing so, the lives of those who received it from me may have been greatly impacted. Because God lavishes me with flavorful buckets of mercy, I am able to turn around and pour it onto others.

Dear merciful Father, may we live beside the well of mercy and may our buckets be constantly raised and lowered into Your life- freeing water. Lord, yes. There is no greater love than merciful love. Help us remember this, O Lord. Father, we can know we are well -watered when we are saturated in mercy and the runoff seeps deep into the roots of everyone nearby. Be generous with Your extra bucket, Your double portion. May God bless the precious hearts of those who read this, and display Your mighty power within them for all to see and proclaim Your name. In Jesus, amen.

Power to Rise Above

My late teenage years and early to mid-twenties are almost unbearable to recall. With all the baggage that I carried, it is a wonder that I managed to move more than three feet in a day. I owned hefty grudges and was broken by the weight of the massive chips mounted on my shoulders. There are numerous valid devastations I can claim; it was not all overblown drama. It was, however, my attachment to the things that scarred that kept me chained inside a prison cell. I did not have the strength to get out of my prison on my own, and barely a desire. I existed under monuments of pain that I observed daily and paid pathetic homage to.

In those years, I was betrayed, abandoned, and wounded over and over again. Unfortunately, I was lacking strength and clarity in those years, which led me on a search for approval and acceptance. The desire to be loved more drove my decisions and inspired me to make many many poor ones. To go into more detail would require me to throw some people under the bus, to call out some perpetrators, and to expose some of my loved ones to painful truths that they might rather not know. But know this: my actions led me to loss. They led me to shame. They led me to loneliness. My sin made its mark all over my heart.

My heavenly Father's supernatural freeing of me from those chains is the crux of His story in me. It is nothing short of miraculous. I never had the power on my own to bust through those bars and shed the chains. I surrendered and bowed down. He busted the chains that bound me and broke me free. By His power, I did rise above. I continue to face trials and endure sufferings, and He continues to offer me the power to rise above hate, envy, pride, revenge, betrayal, and gossip. He is just that powerful, and it is miraculous every time.

We don't have to be defeated through loss, pain, and trials. We have options in the midst of our suffering. We can remain wounded and stay down, continuing to live in defeat. Jesus wasn't merely wounded on the cross; He was terminated. But even that did not keep Him down. By God's power, He rose. We too can rise above the sufferings we endure. We can approach the well of living waters for the power to rise above. He will not leave our buckets empty when we seek for them to be filled.

His incomparably great power is for those of us who believe—the same power that conquered the grave and raised up Christ from the dead. Because He was raised, we can rise. Paul wrote to the church in Ephesus,

> I keep asking that the God of our Lord Jesus Christ, the glorious Father, may give you the Spirit of wisdom and revelation, so that you may know him better. I pray also that the eyes of your heart may be enlightened in order that you may know the hope to which he has called you, the riches of his glorious inheritance in the saints, and his incomparably great *power for us* who believe. *That power is like the working of his mighty strength*, which he exerted in Christ when he *raised* him from the dead and seated him at his right hand in the heavenly realms." (Ephesians 1:17-20, NIV, emphasis added)

Paul inspires me to be passionate about encouraging others. I pray these words encourage us to recognize the power we have in Christ. We do not have to stay down in defeat, even if our wounds were self-inflicted. In Him we have the power to rise above. May we claim that today.

It may seem impossible to walk both in power and in humility. We are called over and over and over again throughout Scripture to be humble. So it is not my hope that we view the power of God within us the way that the world views power. The power He pours into us is miraculous indeed, but it is for His glory alone. As always, the buckets of power He pours into us are meant to be a blessing to us and also to bless a watching world. His design is that He would be displayed in each of us and presented as an olive branch to a world desperately in need of peace.

While I grasp this understanding, I have fallen into the temptation to believe that these conquering powers are my own. Even though it pains me to confess such foolishness, I'll share a story of a crown I tried to wear. I had been in a women's Bible study for about three years, meeting regularly with the same group of women and feeling every ounce of the blessing that it was—and remains. Once we'd gotten to know each other well, it was clear that we all had junk, drama, trials, suffering, and pain (a very unlikely commonality among women, right?). We were dealing with our lives with as much grace from God as we could possibly claim, and yet things were getting tougher.

One of my Bible study sisters and I, who are both especially vocal, didn't hesitate to state our desires for Jesus to come quick and for Satan to hit the road. At that time, there seemed to be an extreme amount of warfare going on around us all. We knew we were in Christ and that our testimonies had value in the heavenlies, so we were not surprised to be under attack, but we did seem to forget temporarily *who* could stop it. In church, of all places, on a Sunday morning, I ran into my dear, equally vocal friend. We quickly discussed our enemy and right there in a holy house I proceeded to make a threat to Satan.

I'll be honest. My target was a sensitive area of his anatomy, if you catch what I'm tossing. It was inappropriate on so many levels. I cringe right now even thinking about it. But it was also mostly for fun, this banter between she and me. After all, we were in our home church, and we were feeling empowered.

The problem is that this power from God to rise above isn't like a weapon. Well, it is, but it isn't. God doesn't hand us a sword and then leave us alone. God *is* the sword. *Do you see the difference?* I'm not in battle in this world with a few tools of my own on which to rely. He is my weapon and defense. He is my sword, my armor, my wisdom, my helmet, and my shield. He is the conqueror. Not me. Let us not forget that all the glory belongs to God, and in His power is ours: "Finally, be strong in the Lord and in his mighty power. Put on the full armor of God, so that you can take your stand against the devil's schemes. For our struggle is not against flesh and blood, but against the rulers, against the authorities, against the powers of this dark world and against the spiritual forces of evil in the heavenly realms" (Ephesians 6:10-12, NIV).

Shortly after my threatened assault on Satan, it was as if the power went out of me—and my friend, too, for laughing at the crown on my head instead of lovingly whacking it off of me. The attacks got more vicious, more cunning, and more devastating. Please don't misunderstand. I do not believe that God was punishing me for parading around power that wasn't mine. But I do believe He allowed me to experience what it is like to be left to my own depleted strength, my feeble weakness. I reiterate the bottom line: without His power we are all defeated. Instantly. So I learned very expressly that the approach to victory over Satan is through Christ. I will never again approach that snake on my own.

Scripture says we are foolish to rely on our own manmade cisterns (a tank for storing water), because they break easily. "Be appalled at this, O heavens, and shudder with great horror," declares the Lord. "My people have committed two sins: They have forsaken me, the spring of living water, and have dug their own cisterns, broken cisterns that cannot hold water" (Jeremiah 2:12-13, NIV). This world is out to get us. Scriptures remind us that Satan "prowls around like a roaring lion looking for someone to devour" (I Peter 5:8). In various other places throughout the Word, the devil is also referred to as "the prince of this world" (See John 12; 14; 16). As the prince of this world, the devil is very busy aiming to destroy faithful testimonies from the chain-breaking streams of the living waters, the Lord God Almighty.

I hope you are comforted by the power that is within you to face the battles waged in your life by the prince of this world. May we take up this song of praise by Isaiah:

> Surely God is my salvation; I will trust and not be afraid. The Lord, the Lord, is my strength and my song; he has become my salvation. *With joy you will draw water from the wells of salvation.* In that day you will say: "Give thanks to the Lord, call on his name; make known among the nations what he has done, and proclaim that his name is exalted. Sing to the Lord, for he has done glorious things; let this be known to all the world." (Isaiah 12:2-5, NIV, emphasis added)

The wells of salvation are wells that we draw from today (and daily) because of the redemptive blood of Christ. Every bend of the knee in prayer is a trek to the wells. Every prayer is a bucket raised. Every act of love and service cleanses your spirit in water that purifies—His living water.

> *Oh, sweet, precious Lord, may You ever encourage us in hope that is centered at the well of Your living waters. May our love be lifted high to You while in meek humility we tap into the powers You long to pour into our spirit. And because of Your glorious resurrection, in You we rise above. In the saving name of Jesus, amen.*

∾

Power to Discern

Paul wrote to the Philippians, "And this I pray, that your love may abound still more and more in real knowledge and all discernment, so that you may approve the things that are excellent, in order to be sincere and blameless until the day of Christ; having been filled with the fruit of righteousness which comes through Jesus Christ, to the glory and praise of God" (Philippians I:9-II, NASB).

Discernment is akin to wisdom and knowledge. Scripture says far more about wisdom than about discernment. The book of Proverbs practically dissects the innards of a wise person and a foolish person and props them all up in display for the masses. The goal is not a worldly wisdom but a wisdom that can come only from God. The *Holman Hebrew-Greek Key Word Study Bible* (NASB) defines *discernment* with words such as *judgment, sense,* and *understanding* as well as *distinguish* and *decide.*

I was taught that discernment is the ability to determine right from wrong in the context of relating to God, which isn't simple. Some rights and wrongs are plain and simple. It is wrong to drive under the influence of drugs, alcohol, and mind-altering medications because of the exponentially higher probability of causing an accident. Other rights and wrongs are fuzzy and would be best faced in prayer and fellowship, such as making career changes, confronting a conflict, or raising and disciplining children.

Christians are shaped to want to know which decisions are going to keep us in the will of God. We want to remain as upright and straightforward as we can in this journey. Discernment is a gift from God ; it is wisdom to live, lead, and make decisions that are in His will. In the book of Hebrews, discernment is described as a quality or characteristic that is likely to be found in someone with a mature faith. As Hebrews 5:14 says, "Solid food is for the mature, who because of practice have their senses trained to discern good and evil." This was a daunting piece of information for me in the early part of my Christian journey. While I wanted to know everything of God, I knew that I knew very little. I immediately felt like I was behind. I was twenty-nine when I accepted Christ, so some of my friends were years (and decades) ahead of me. They knew the Bible like the backs of their hands. How could I possibly catch up to what it took them a lifetime to learn?

Well, God gave me great peace about wisdom and discernment early on when I studied spiritual gifts in I Corinthians 12 with a small community group. I still find comfort in this chapter. It makes it clear that the Holy Spirit is going to cause a certain giftedness (or multiple spiritual gifts) to fall on all Christians. We were created to be alike in our faith but diversified in our gifts. We are known as *the body* of Christ. As with a physical body, a hand has different functions than a foot. Your spiritual gifts may vary greatly from mine. One spiritual gift is the ability to distinguish between good and bad. The word *distinguish* has the same meaning as *discern*. But what I love about the definition of *distinguish* is that it is "the *power* to discern between good and evil."

Not everyone has the gift of discernment, but we all face situations in which some discernment is needed. We all face evil disguised as good. What I want for us to see is that this *power* to discern is available to us even if it is not one of our personal strengths. It may not fall upon us as quickly as we would like, but in every decision we ever face, we can approach the well with our buckets and ask for a fill of discernment.

Sometimes the right choice is hiding like a mystery among many options. What do we do when so many options *seem* fair and reasonable? How can we know our decision is honoring to God? There may be more than one right choice, but I believe we honor Him most when we seek understanding and ask to be able to distinguish what is good from what is evil. In seeking God's power, we can make choices based on discernment from His Spirit, because He will help us determine what is good and what He desires to do through us. I hope you find encouragement from the apostle Paul in what he wrote to the church in Colossae: "that their hearts may be encouraged, having been knit together in love, and attaining to all the wealth that comes from *the full assurance of understanding*, resulting in a true knowledge of God's mystery, that is, Christ Himself, in whom are hidden all the treasures of wisdom and knowledge" (Colossians 2:2-3, emphasis added).

According to this verse, the mysteries of God are hidden in Jesus; they are glorious treasures of wisdom and discernment. What I love most about this Scripture is that it says our hearts are "knit together in love." God will bless us with understanding when we seek it—not just understanding, but the full assurance of it. A peace. A comfort. He wants to fill our buckets with every good thing from Him. He will fill us with the very portion we need when we need it. He doesn't want us to fail to approach the well with our buckets so desperate for filling. Oh, how He loves us! His living water is all we need.

> *Mighty God, may we bless Your precious name when it leaves our lips. May we desire You more and more for the wondrous mysteries hidden in Christ. In Your glorious name, may the discovery and full assurance be found at the well. Fill our hearts with all the fullness we can have of You, O Lord. In Jesus's name, amen.*

Power to Persevere

There are not enough coffee beans in the world to sustain the refills that would be necessary if we were to sit together and discuss all the ways life hurts. The opportunities to experience devastation are simply endless. People commit wrongs against one another; freak things happen randomly; and our own personal colossal mistakes can be devastating. There is heartache and sorrow around every corner. Life is so hard!

If you are anything at all like me, you may have spent periods of life when the bad far outweighed the good. And it may have left you wondering what the purpose was. Life can feel like a series of streets decorated with Dead End signs and critical No U-Turn warnings. The worst is when you find yourself at the dark end of the street with *both* signs posted. You can't turn around, and there is nowhere to go. I have been there at least a dozen times, and nothing feels worse. Those signs have many names: Cancer, Affair, Unemployment, Infertility, Divorce, Betrayal, and Addiction, just to name a few.

When you or I face what seems like a no U-turn dead end, we would rather be anywhere than there. I know what it feels like for my hope to evaporate into thin air and for my spirit to deflate like a flat tire. In these dark times, we can once again approach the King on His throne and ask for His provision of power. He longs to empower us to persevere and to do so confidently. Hebrews 10:35-36 says, "Do not throw away your confidence; it will be richly rewarded. You need to persevere so that when you have done the will of God, you will receive what he has promised." He has promised victory and eternity to those who believe and love Him.

Whether you are a long-time believer in Christ or you are still trying to figure out if faith is worth a prayer, perseverance is necessary when you walk (or crawl) through difficult situations. There is glory in the tough times, and the tougher the times, the greater the glory that will be revealed. In this sense, we should *want* to experience trials because of the transformation that God will orchestrate in us through them. This will look different for each of us, but no matter what valleys God asks you to journey through, embrace your trials and suffering. If you will cling tightly to the Word of the Lord when you are suffering, through Him you will persevere. He empowers us to persevere when we place our hope in Him—not only to persevere, but to find joy in the suffering.

This may be the point when you want to slam the book closed because it sounds ridiculous to you, but please travel through the Word with me again. I've asked you to consider that Jesus is the spring of living water, and we may approach Him in prayer as if He is a deep well with an abundance of provision, willing to fill our buckets. Through His Spirit, He will provide the power to persevere, and He will make it possible for us to find joy amidst our trials and suffering. James wrote, "Consider it pure joy, my brothers, whenever you face trials of many kinds, because you know that the testing of your faith develops perseverance. Perseverance must finish its work so that you may be mature and complete, not lacking anything" (James 1:2-4, NIV).

God does not enjoy watching us endure the hardest things in life. However, if we seek Him and love Him, He gets great joy out of using our trials to develop in us the ability to persevere. Did you see the gem in the verse above? Perseverance leads us to completion, and in completion we lack nothing. Oh, how I dare to dream of a day when you and I lack nothing.

It is during our perseverance that we are sifted. It is by persevering that we are molded and refined. Only through trials that ignite a persevering spirit within us will God perform miraculous change in the core of who we are. It is through trials and perseverance that He will extract the unwanted stuff inside of us, like dross from silver. When silver is heated in a refining fire, the dross (unwanted stuff) bubbles to the surface and can be removed. All that's left is precious metal worth working with, worth shaping into something beautiful by the silversmith; *the refiner*. Proverbs 25:4 says, "Remove the dross from the silver, and out comes material for the silversmith." God uses our trials to purify us.

Being able to look into our fiery trial or to reflect back on one should stir us to feel some degree of joy in knowing that we are worth refining. We are precious in the sight of the Lord, and He is making us beautiful. He refines us to bring about spiritual maturity in us so that we can be complete. He will refine, mature, and complete us for His kingdom of heaven. Do you see yourself in the big picture of heaven? Do you realize that you are part of the economy that makes heaven so rich? *Yes, you.* Because you love Him, He is at work in you. You are being refined and empowered by Him to make a positive impact on the kingdom. You are His most natural resource. "Now to him who is able to do immeasurably more than all we ask or imagine, according to his power that is at work within us, to him be glory in the church and in Christ Jesus throughout all generations, for ever and ever! Amen" (Ephesians 3:20-21, NIV).

Don't give up. Do not stop moving, hoping, and loving. Do not doubt that you can and will persevere when your life is surrendered to the will of God. You will persevere by His power because He has promised to complete the good work that He has begun in you. You will persevere by His power because you are part of His kingdom economy. You will persevere because His Spirit is guiding you and there are lamps along your path. You will persevere because the victory is already His, all of your battles have been won, and the end of your story is glory. Hardship and trials will come. Through them you will be refined and matured. It will hurt, but joy belongs to you. God will never send you away from His well without providing what you need in your bucket.

> *Sweet Father, please carry us through with strength to persevere. Cast Your Spirit on us now to inject us with the utter confidence to know that You have gone before us, that Your love is enough, and that in You we have no reason to fear. You have called us to persevere in Your great name, and we want that power in abundance. Lead us to be joyful in trials and to be reminded that suffering has its purpose in this journey. You are Lord of all, and You make no mistakes. We are not here by accident. Father God, etch this truth on our hearts. In Jesus, amen.*

Power to Love

Love is so much more than just a word. It is more than a warm, fuzzy feeling. More than butterflies in the tummy and more than staccato heartbeat rhythms. More than warm embraces and hands held under a shade tree. More than the breath of a newborn baby. It is much deeper. Love is our profound attachment to people and their hopes, feelings, and desires. It is a shared connection to others' pain and a desperation for their happiness and longevity. Love is action and emotion.

To even begin to hope that we could love the way that God does, our love must travel through Him first. You and I are not ever going to be capable of loving like Him without Him. His love is perfect, void of ulterior motives. His love gives life, restores brokenness, and fills emptiness. His love conquers death, lays the foundation for eternity on streets of gold, and reaches to depths that do not make sense. His love builds up and tears down. His is the only *unconditional* love. We cannot embody the whole of His perfect love. His love meter remains constantly at the highest reading. Ours fluctuates, but through His Spirit, He empowers us with His love. Yes, He loves us, but He intends for us to love others with a Christlike love, and He alone makes it possible. Easy? No. Possible? Yes.

Maybe you have noticed that there are many unlovable people in this world? Some of them are made famous by their acts of hatred, their characteristics of entitlement, or their abuse of authority. We can call to mind countless hateful people in this world, ranging from criminals to political figures to corporate leaders. We can point to "self-serving" neighbors, bullies, malicious competitors, and "mean girls" of all ages. It is so hard to love these people, and yet Scripture makes it clear that we are to love them first: "But I tell you who hear me: Love your enemies, do good to those who hate you, bless those who curse you, pray for those who mistreat you" (Luke 6:27-28, NIV).

Furthermore, loving lovable people is nice but not commendable. Luke, the companion to Paul the Apostle, explained that we don't get "credit" for loving the people who are easy to love: "If you love those who love you, what credit is that to you? Even sinners love those who love them. And if you do good to those who are good to you, what credit is that to you? Even sinners do that" (Luke 6:32-33, NIV). It seems harsh, yet as I search for the truth of this in my heart, I begin to understand.

It helps for me to think of my children in this case and to examine my role as their mom. Things I reward my children for come to mind as well as things I do not reward. I have, in a sense, commanded them to meet certain expectations. I do not reward them for getting dressed, because getting dressed is a simple, basic, necessary task. It goes without saying that it must be done. If one of them were to approach me in the morning asking for a "treat" because they got dressed, I'd pretty much reply, "Nice try," because getting dressed isn't an exceptional behavior.

Neither is it remarkable to love the people who make us happy and warm our hearts. Performing obvious, easy acts of love is not worthy of honorable mention. It just isn't. Not that our love doesn't impact lives, because it can, and it does matter to everyone who receives it. However, the challenging command is to love everyone, no matter the circumstances and no matter how difficult. This may seem senseless to us, and it may bring a sting of pain, yet we are commanded to love unlovable people. This is simply how God works.

Jesus displayed astonishing acts of love over and over. He extended His love, mercy, compassion, grace, and forgiveness on the very worst, most hated people in Scripture. He didn't reserve His love only for those who followed Him. That would have been easy and of no credit to Him. He taught that the most grotesque human beings are most in need of His purifying love, and He showed us by His example that the most twisted and heinous people can be redeemed and made new. New Testament Scripture cites examples of lepers, tax collectors, and prostitutes. In our world today, this translates to drug dealers, child abusers, terrorists, thieves, rapists, sexual predators, and drunk drivers. This command applies to property squatters, people who spew hatred, rude neighbors, and coworkers who take credit for our work. It does not eliminate the boss who promises you a promotion in exchange for a sexual favor or the best friend who sleeps with your spouse.

God does not call us to be doormats to be stomped on. He does encourage us through His Word to understand that the love we receive from Him is as undeserved and as unlikely, in the grand scheme of things, as the love we are called to express toward the most unlovable human beings of our time. It is a reminder to us that in grace He has overlooked (forgiven) our sins. Because Christ does not withhold love from us as a form of punishment, we also are not to punish others by withholding love. We all deserve for God to withhold His love from us, because we all have sinned and fall short of His glory (Romans 3:23).

The only difference between us and nonbelievers on death row is forgiveness. You and I (death row or not) are forgiven because we have surrendered. Actions do not set us apart. Behavior does not set us apart. The number of times the word *love* has parted from our lips does not set us apart. We are set apart only by the mercy and grace that leads to forgiveness. So what does God ask of us? *To love.* There is no place in this journey for revenge or hatred. Cold hearts do not belong. Not reaching out to love the unlovable is like dropping your anchor in the pit of hell and proclaiming it as your personal residence. There is nothing safe about unforgiveness. Hating our perpetrators cannot glorify God.

We have been perpetrators against Him, and yet He has forgiven freely. We have abused and denied God. We have twisted His words and disobeyed His commands. We have turned a deaf ear, and we have crucified Him. We have utterly betrayed Him, and we have loved sin. Every last one of us. No exclusions. No exceptions. The sins committed against us are not worse than the sins committed against Christ; therefore, we are to extend love and forgiveness as He has modeled by loving and forgiving us, His trespassers. Jesus said, "Love your enemies, do good to them, and lend to them without expecting to get anything back. Then your reward will be great, and you will be sons of the Most High, because he is kind to the ungrateful and wicked. Be merciful, just as your Father is merciful" (John 6:35-36).

How, how, how, oh, how do we love the ones we'd rather classify with the cockroaches? This I know: on our own we have not an ounce of power to do it. I do not believe in forgive and forget. I believe in forgive and remember enough to be fully aware of the glory of God Almighty. His power in us can accomplish this. But I'm not sure we can grab a bucket, mosey on up to the well, and expect to receive this one. We might need a village, joined hand in hand, with buckets hanging from all of our extremities like Christmas trees. In fact, we may not even be able to walk to the well. We may need to crawl on our knees and elbows, as if going into combat. Or we may need to be carried by others whose love buckets have already been filled. No matter how we get there, if there was ever a well worthy of falling head over heels into, it is this one.

The most blessed and precious experiment I have ever conducted during my faith journey has involved a love bucket. You see, I know how to hate. I have experience in hatred, and I knew that it was slowing killing me. The root of bitterness was strangling every good fiber in me that was struggling to grow up through it. I remembered an old song sung by a dear friend of mine, Brown Bannister. Brown is a record producer and songwriter, and he has a peaceful, soothing voice. He lived across the street from me in my childhood. I was nuts about him and his sweet family. Because of our friendship, I was given one of Brown's records when it was released. I played it over and over from beginning to end for many years. To this day (thirty years later), I still sing a song that was adapted from Psalm 51:10: "Create in me a clean heart, O Lord my God; and renew a right spirit within me."

What began in my ears as the soothing comfort of a soft, harmonious voice became in me a longing to live my life for God. Without Him, what in me is clean? This song is a prayer God intended for me; He wants me to understand that He will clean my heart if I ask Him, and He will renew His Spirit within me. This prayer doesn't say, "God, please give me more love"; it begs, "Lord, please clean my heart." Instead of asking God to give me more love, I asked Him to remove the junk.

Isn't "junk removal" the essence of cleaning? When I clean out my garage, sweeping doesn't usually cut it. I have to box up the garbage and the excess and get rid of it. Just by clearing out the clutter, even without using soap, it is far cleaner. So I prayed continually, "O Lord, create in me a clean heart. Take out the junk and all of that mess formed by bitterness and hate. Please remove the stones that were stacked with each wound. Please tear down the monuments of anger I have daily observed and the chains of betrayals that hold me hostage. Please pack up and ship out the weapons I have formed in my thoughts and that rest on my tongue. Please dissolve the hate that is hiding in the darkest corners of my heart!" He heard my prayer and blessed me with the removal of the root of bitterness and the poison of hatred.

When God cleanses our hearts and renews our spirits, this is what happens: His love in us has room to blossom and bloom. Our hearts are overtaken with love instead of the junk that once dwelled there. Loving others is no longer a conscious decision but a natural reaction in Christ. This is glory. It is then that His love moves through us to reach a hurting world. It is then that others see Him within us. It is then that someone with darkness in her soul might surrender to good instead of evil. It is then that a terrorist, a rapist, a thief, or an abuser of power might start to believe he needs redemption and can have it. Judge not. Love much.

When your heart is clean and your spirit is renewed, your heart becomes a wellspring of life. Proverbs 4:23 says, "Above all else, guard your heart, for it is the wellspring of life." The *New Oxford American Dictionary* (online) defines *wellspring* as "an original, bountiful source of something." We are to guard our hearts, because our hearts are the original, bountiful source of whatever we have to offer. We are to offer love. God will cleanse our hearts and renew our spirits so that our bountiful source will be love instead of every other alternative. I love that this same verse in Proverbs in the NASB translation says, "Watch over your heart with all diligence, for from it flow the springs of life." That's right, the very wellspring that is our heart is made to pour out springs of life. Isn't that just another way of saying that the living waters (that is, Christ Jesus) flow from our very own hearts? Yes, it is. Romans 5:5 says, "And hope does not disappoint us, because God has poured out his love into our hearts by the Holy Spirit, whom he has given us."

We can escape the prisons we lock ourselves into every time we hold a grudge and refuse to forgive. Love is the key. And "we are more than conquerors through him who loved us" (Romans 8:37b).

Lord, may our hearts be cleansed by You daily, that You would make us new and restore our spirits each time we seek this blessing from You. Lord, may we humbly receive Your power to love, that the power of Your love would spring forth outside of us and into the hearts of those who have dwelled in darkness and whose actions have dealt countless evil hands. By Your Spirit, Lord, may we be miraculously transformed into lovers instead of haters and forgivers instead of punishers, and may we be freed from our own evil so that we may freely love like You do. Your name is too mighty to utter, Your glory is too powerful to claim, and Your love is too perfect to fathom, yet we seek everything we may be allowed to see. May we live up to Your commands and rejoice in Your rewards. In Jesus we ask, amen.

PART II

~ His Garden ~

Within a life lived centered at the well abides a soul longing for and receiving a spiritual bath and the chance to grow. The muck we've rolled in is tenderly and meticulously wiped away. Years of caked-on sin and pain begin to chip off. Devastation is soaked and rubbed until its visibility is more like a faded stain, and less like a bold tattoo. He planted you. You are growing into a child again. You are being made new. Your agony and grief are falling away. Baby, you look good!

CHAPTER 4

A NEW CREATION

radically transformed

Because of the stark and dramatic difference within me, revelation has settled into my bones. Jesus doesn't just want to save me; He wants to renovate me with love. He wants this for all of us. He doesn't view us as blades of grass, blending into the scenery, but rather as a blossom, each one of us standing out. He wants us to be different—not only different from what we once were, but also different from the masses of those who do not claim Him as Savior. He wants us to grow and bloom.

I am reminded regularly that a significant number of people do not believe in God, have no interest in Jesus, and think that those of us who do are off our rockers. I see, hear, and read it and am regularly confronted by it. There are endless rants by atheists on blogs and social-media outlets that are written with hatred and disdain for people of faith. Conversations find me and occur with people who believe that there is one god with many names and that everyone is saved, or that there is no heaven. I've heard it and seen it all, and I know that Christian beliefs are rejected by many.

My mind has explored many different belief systems, and I have wrestled with doubt. But what reeled me in every single time was the undeniable witness of my own radical transformation. I have felt and followed promptings of the Holy Spirit only to be immeasurably blessed by experiences and outcomes filled with peace, comfort, and joy. After relying on myself for twenty-nine years and getting nowhere, I came to the end of myself and to the beginning of a relationship with God through Christ Jesus. And everything changed. Some of the changes were immediate and significant. It was virtually impossible for me to ignore the radical differences in my character, passions, and actions after I dared to believe.

This is why so many Christians are fine if nonbelievers want to think we are crazy or stupid or weak. In *hope*, like Abraham's hope, we have believed in what we have not seen. Because of our belief, we see, hear, feel, know, and experience the presence of God. Genuine belief becomes authentic faith, which leads to knowing. We cannot let go of that. We will not! Radical transformation is a miracle that we happily sing about as we are sent out into the world to share His love. Some people want to be *convinced* before they will choose to believe. Those who are called Christians first believe and then are convinced.

So, if you are reading and you believe the Word of God is true about Jesus, about salvation, and about heaven—then believe it all. Believe His promises. Trust in His precepts and commands. Believe in the power that He says is yours. Believe that He will not leave you or forsake you. Believe that He will finish what He started. Believe that He has a purpose and a plan for you and that His Spirit resides within your heart as a counselor, friend, and teacher. Believe that you can know peace that surpasses understanding. Believe that the way you live your life has kingdom consequences, heaven is real, love is a verb, and faith without deeds is dead. Believe in double portions of blessings. Believe that your heart is a wellspring of life and that in Christ your thirst will always be quenched. Believe that His way is better than yours and that all your battles have already been won. Believe that He doesn't want you to worry or fear and that He will comfort those feelings. Believe that sin is a hindrance to life and to heaven and that He can strengthen you to overcome. Believe that you are a light in this world and that you have a responsibility to illuminate the truth of who He is and how to know Him. Believe that He can redeem and restore anyone. Believe in love, fellowship, prayer, worship, and praise, and believe that every page of Scripture matters. Believe that He isn't through with you yet.

No matter where you stand today, what you face, and how you got there, it is never too late to be radically transformed. Don't get comfortable, and don't stand still. Get up and move. Seek. Love. Hope. Pray. Serve. Go. Trust. Expand. Grow.

I know for sure that your life was designed by God to be lived for Him. We tend to make life personal and to focus inward. If we were to zoom out and take a grand look at the massiveness of this thing, I believe we would see in simplicity that this life isn't about this life. *This life isn't about this life*. We have made it about us. Now let us make it about Him instead—and not just Him but His entire plan.

If we continue to huddle up in holy cocoons, remaining within the boundaries of our comfort zones, we fail to be the blessing that He has designed us to be. Yes, our families are important and we have been called to "raise up our children in the way that they should go" (Proverbs 22:6). But where does it say in the Bible that we are permitted to wait to serve the kingdom (outside of family) until our babies are grown?

Jesus did not teach His disciples to focus on career first. In fact, He asked them to leave everything to follow Him. *Everything*. He did not teach them to prioritize their families and then just fit Him in whenever they had time left over. Quite the contrary. Jesus's words throughout the Gospels indicate that His ministry takes priority over our own desires. We often convince ourselves that in our present season of life God will permit us to prioritize our family over His kingdom, although Scripture never says that it is okay for us to place our agenda above His. (Our family can certainly be *a* priority, but not *the* priority.)

Most of us don't like being told that our spiritual priorities are out of whack, but just where in Scripture are we given permission to focus only on ourselves? God didn't design us to give Him thanks at the end of the day in a simple memorized prayer for three minutes before bedtime. He designed us to follow Him, and by doing this, to be in a relationship with Him. And where is He going that we should follow? He is going to the ends of the earth to shepherd His lost sheep. Through us, He is sharing gospel truth, and He is preparing our home in heaven.

See, heaven is our actual home—not earth. When you crawl into bed to close your eyes and rest, you are not at home. Nothing that you have today is going to last forever, and nothing that you have today is perfect. There is no relationship that can complete you and no dream that can fulfill the desires of your heart to the fullest. Most of us are chasing "someday." We are tricked into living in constant search of completion, wholeness, and perfection through worldly things that cannot keep the lies they promise. Completion, wholeness, and perfection await us, but not in this world.

Let me ask you this: Does your family plan vacations? What do you go through to get ready for that vacation? A lot of things have to be pulled together for a vacation to happen. The truth is, preparing for a vacation can be quite time consuming, tedious, and complicated. Simply, we cannot just hop on a plane and go wherever we want without planning. There is the money part and the organization and packing, and then the actual act of travel, whether it is by car, plane, train, boat, or foot. Do you have pets that have to be taken care of while you are away? Maybe some bills need to be paid while you are gone, plants to be watered, lawn to be mowed, mail to be collected—and you need someone to keep an eye on your home.

I know some people who spend their entire year looking forward to a vacation. Some even post an official countdown on their blogs and social-media pages. For some, it is the greatest part of their year, so they look forward to it with excitement and eager anticipation. The whole year of labor and work makes it all worth it to experience the retreat, the stunning views, or the expressions of joy on their children's faces.

So, we know how to look forward, how to anticipate and get excited. We know how to count down, and we know that we cannot accomplish any of it without some degree of planning. We know how to plan our worldly adventures. But we fail over and over again to look forward to heaven and to plan accordingly. Our error is in failing to understand that this life is fleeting. "Show me, O Lord," the psalmist wrote, "my life's end and the number of my days; let me know how fleeting is my life. You have made my days a mere handbreadth; the span of my years is as nothing before you. Each man's life is but a breath" (Psalm 39:4-5, NIV). We spend our lives trying to carve out our own worldly idea of "heaven" and to experience it in the here and now instead of realizing that this life is a mission, not a vacation. This life is for loving others to Christ.

There is no system of reward or pleasure that we can implement here that He hasn't already far outdone in the heavenly realms. Why do we need bucket lists? Why do we need to establish a list of things to do, see, or experience on this earth before we die, as if it would make our lives complete? We treat death like it is the end instead of the beginning. We live with regrets instead of with expectations of glory. Why do we do this? Are we not reading the Scriptures, or do we not believe them? Are we confused about heaven?

We are alive today in a culture that encourages an inward focus and we are perpetually driven toward discovering how to make life better for ourselves. Our senses of urgency are for family, career, health, and finances. We seem to lack a sense of urgency for the kingdom of God. Who of us is losing sleep because someone is lost? Who of us is *as* worried about the salvation of our neighbor as we are about the salvation of our own children? I don't believe we have made a conscious decision to ignore the priorities of Christ, but we have effectively set them aside. This is why we should so desperately want to be overhauled from the inside out in a radical transformation like the one described in Colossians: "Since, then, you have been raised with Christ, set your hearts on things above, where Christ is seated at the right hand of God. Set your minds on things above, not on earthly things. For you died, and your life is now hidden with Christ in God" (3:1-4, NIV).

If we are living first for ourselves, we haven't been radically transformed, and this should frighten us a bit. I ask you urgently and fervently to seek wisdom here. Jesus tells us, "It is easier for a camel to go through the eye of a needle than for someone who is rich* to enter the kingdom of God" (Mark 10:25, NIV). Jesus also warns us firmly that the road to life (everlasting) is very narrow; that there are true and false disciples; and that fruitless lives will not be welcomed into the kingdom of heaven:

"Not everyone who says to me, 'Lord, Lord,' will enter the kingdom of heaven, but only the one who does the will of my Father who is in heaven. Many will say to me on that day, 'Lord, Lord, did we not prophesy in your name and in your

---

In Mark 10 is an account of a rich man who approached Jesus and asked him how to inherit eternal life. First, Jesus reminded the young rich man of several biblical commands. Finally, he told him to sell everything and give to the poor (v. 21), proclaiming that when he did so, he would have treasure in heaven. Next we are told that the man hung his head in sorrow, presumably because he did not want to forfeit his wealth.

This is just one of numerous examples of Jesus and the disciples teaching that we are to serve the poor, the widows, and the orphans. If we were to note every single instance in Scripture where we are told (and examples are set) to help the poor and needy, we might concur that it is mandatory. And I personally believe (as I feel God has shown me) that this is a significant aspect of our radical transformation. Whether we can be generous with what we have been given and whether we genuinely care about the needs of orphans, widows, and those in poverty is an indication of whether we have been transformed. I don't believe that God cares to gauge how much we have as much as He pays attention to how readily we give. The young rich man spoken of in Mark 10 was very fond of his wealth and possessions. He didn't seem to want to part with them. He was treating this life on earth today (that day) as if it held more value to him than the eternal life in heaven that is promised.

According to data from the World Bank, half of the earth's population lives on less than two dollars per day. Half of those live on less than 1.25 per day. America is the sixth wealthiest country on the planet. Simply put, those of us who can afford to go out to eat once per month are wealthy. Those of us who live in a house and have two cars are in the top 5 percent, even if we are living paycheck to paycheck and without a savings account.

If your heart hasn't been broadened to give of your resources and to serve those in poverty, you can ask God to work on this in you, and He will.

name drive out demons and in your name perform many miracles?' Then I will tell them plainly, 'I never knew you. Away from me, you evildoers!'" (Matthew 7:21-23)

Did you notice in the final verse that a person living a fruitless life is an "evildoer"? A heart surrendered to Him will result in radical transformation, because genuine faith produces obedience. A disciple willing to make all of humankind a priority rather than to idolize immediate family will walk in light with the Lord of all creation. A soul who answers the call to take up a cross daily is eternal. May we not be guilty of thinking that this life was made for our personal bucket lists. We are co-missioners. Heaven is the vacation that we are to focus our hearts and efforts on. Heaven is *the bucket!*

In case you are wondering, know that I have not lived up to what I have written here. I am not a master of taking up a cross daily or living for others. I struggle with idolizing my family and prioritizing from the inside out instead of the outside in. I'm worried that I could be one of the evildoers and Jesus may look at me on judgment day and tell me, "Away from me. I never knew you." How desperately I do not want that to be my story or yours. So we are going to explore growing in Christ. We are going to explore this radical transformation that He promises is worth the cross we carry.

Scripture uses themes to teach us. The divine, inspired Word of God is beautiful and creative. It is metaphorical, tangible, flavorful, and rich in wisdom. As we have already seen, God has used the theme of water to inspire us toward glory; He is living water. We have seen that He is a life source that springs forth. I love that He gave us some pictures to paint in our minds about the power that He offers us, and that we can receive these powers from Him by approaching the well of His life-giving provision, where He will never fail to fill us with what we need. I deeply praise Him for that. He has taught us already that He is the way, the truth, and the light; that He is in us and shines through us; and that if we center our lives at the well, by His grace and mercy we will never thirst. Now let us see how His Word has inspired more metaphors for living, that we are like plants, gardens, vines, and trees.

As I continue to write in my flawed, human understanding, I pray this:

> *May the Spirit of Christ move upon you to grasp the wisdom that can only be from Him and that you will bloom into the full scope of beauty He gives as you reflect His love into the world and as you glow with His light into the darkness where your path intersects with those who are lost, searching for hope. Lord, God of wisdom and wonder, please bless our journey. We shout Your name, Jesus. Amen.*

CHAPTER 5

PLANTED IN HIS GARDEN

You don't have to make it far in Scripture to see that God is a gardener. In Genesis 2 we are taught that God planted a garden in the East, in Eden (v. 8). We read on to learn that God Himself made all kinds of trees grow in His beautiful garden. We're told some trees were pleasing to the eyes, while others produced good food.

Many believe that Moses was probably the writer of the book of Genesis. We know from Scriptures that Moses and God were very close. They were friends: "the Lord would speak to Moses face to face, as one speaks to a friend" (Exodus 33:11, NIV). I believe that Moses had it on good authority from the God of all creation to write out the creation story. What I love about the garden sequence is this: God did not speak the garden into being during the first six days of creation. After His day of rest, He planted the garden Himself. Maybe that particular day was like a thousand years, but He made shrubs, plants, grass, and trees. So we have reason to believe that God is a master gardener. If gardening is something He so intimately cares about and enjoys, it is no wonder He uses gardening to teach us many things.

A garden cannot flourish without water. Water is a necessity for all living things, including plants. Jesus taught parables of planting seeds, sowing, and reaping. In Mark 4, we are compared to wheat with sheaf that needs sifted. In John 15, Jesus says that He is the vine and we are the branches. In Colossians 2, we are said to be "rooted" in Him. Roots are intertwined and connected in the earth underneath all the beauty and splendor. Something that does not take root cannot grow. Over and over we are taught to bear fruit (Matthew 7; John 15), and we are reminded that, though life is hard, if we will not give up we will reap a harvest (Galatians 6:9). The theme of gardening in God's Word is undeniable.

The first house I owned was an old, little cottage built in 1930. It was tiny but perfectly functional back when my oldest son and I were facing the world together. The exterior of the home was hidden by huge boxwood shrubs that were the size of trees; they hid the splendor and character of our tiny cottage. One of my precious friends offered to help us landscape, including the removal of those giant boxwoods. It took many hours, a lot of manpower, and huge tools to remove those monsters. We had to dig down deep for the roots, and when we located them, we saw that those beasts were like massive tree trunks. Those boxwoods were *deeply* rooted.

For the love of Jesus, I want to be deeply rooted like that. I want Satan to see me and not even bother trying to damage me once he sees the size of my roots and the glory of the vine that I'm attached to. By the end of this journey, if not sooner, we should be so deeply rooted that nothing can harm our connection to Christ. No poison, no crime, no disease, no sin, no circumstance. My back may be permanently damaged from those days of landscaping thirteen years ago, but glory be to the God on high, I've seen something like the roots I want to have. Those shrub roots were severed, but ours can never be.

God is a gardener. He picked us out by hand and chose our location to sprout and grow. He tends to us in every way.

Oh, Father, my prayer is that we will not stand still and fade into the background like a blade of grass, but that we will respond to Your grace with glorious blooms. Tend to us and nurture us, O Lord. May we grow more and more into Your likeness. In Jesus, amen.

❧

Like the Cedars of Lebanon

"The righteous will flourish like a palm tree, they will grow like a cedar of Lebanon; planted in the house of the Lord, they will flourish in the courts of our God. They will still bear fruit in old age, they will stay fresh and green."
Psalm 92:12-14

The term *righteous* was a tremendous stumbling block for me at the beginning of my faith journey. It held a negative connotation, as in "self-righteousness"—people who thought very highly of themselves. And righteousness seemed like a quality attainable only by the holiest of people, like saints, nuns, and religious leaders who actually made it to the grave without a scandal along the way. In other words, *not me*. I did not believe that righteousness could ever apply to me, so I discounted passages like the one above. I dismissed that I could ever be like a cedar of Lebanon, planted in the house of the Lord.

At times like this, biblical resources are vital to one's growth. My *Quest Study Bible* (NIV) offers defining clarity of this daunting term and has allowed me to embrace the righteousness I am destined for. Righteousness: "The fulfillment of the demands of a relationship. God brings believers into a right relation with him, erasing their guilt and crediting righteousness to them and helping them to be devoted to the service of what God says is right." And Romans 1:17 has a lot to say about righteousness: "For in the gospel a righteousness from God is revealed, a righteousness that is by faith from first to last, just as it is written 'The righteous will live by faith'" (NIV).

We can see that the beginning of this word is *right*. A simple explanation of righteousness is that God brings His believers into a right relationship with Him. Faith is credited to believers as righteousness. It seems so simple, because it is so simple. Our faith in Him is more than enough for Him to send His Spirit to move in us and through us to rightly align our hearts with His will, His grace, His endless mercies, and His hope. If you believe in Him, you have been credited with righteousness. Righteousness has nothing to do with how many verses of Scripture you have memorized, how many meals you have served to the hungry, or how many dollars you have donated to charity. You are living in righteousness, a right relationship with God, because of your faith and His grace.

This is glorious news, and now we love the word, right? Right. So let us apply this now back to this psalm we so desperately need to hear. Because of your faith and subsequent righteousness, you are planted in the house of the Lord. You will flourish. You will bear fruit. You will stay fresh and green. Staying fresh and green means you will never die. Eternal life is yours. You will grow strong like a cedar of Lebanon.

There are several references to trees—and specifically the cedars of Lebanon—in Scripture. Lebanon is a Middle Eastern country just to the north of Israel. To its east is Syria and to its west is the Mediterranean Sea. Lebanon is a rocky, mountainous country known for its massive cedar trees. These trees are unique because they grow on rock. Cedar wood is a natural deterrent to insects, and it will not rot, making it virtually impossible to destroy. It is also known for its powerful fragrance. Somehow up on a high rock these trees withstand furious winds and storms without breaking or falling. According to Dr. Joe Temple on www.livingBiblestudies.org, in an article entitled "Like a Cedar Tree," the cedar tree stands very tall and also grows very wide. It is a force to be reckoned with.

Throughout much of Scripture, we see that cedar was very much a part of many important structures, including Solomon's temple. It was considered to be the finest, most durable, and longest lasting material. Some cedars in Lebanon today are believed to be thousands of years old. And there is evidence that they withstand every test of time because they are so deeply rooted. Dr. Temple explains that the deep roots of cedars are nourished by underground springs. Those roots grow down and deep first to quench their thirst. Only by reaching the depths of the springs are they then able to grow up and out. If their roots were not so deeply established, they would tumble, crack, and break, but because of the depths of their rootedness, they are able to grow on rock.

Cedars are rare in quality, useful, fragrant, and strong. And we, my beautiful friends, will grow like the cedars of Lebanon, according to Psalm 92. Together with the body of Christ, in His Spirit, we will grow. We will be deeply rooted. We will carry His fragrance out into the world. We will withstand storms. We will grow wide (not remain narrow), and we will grow up and mature. We will last forever because we will be standing firm on Christ Jesus's solid rock, and we will be fragrant. Amen. As Paul wrote, "Thanks be to God, who always leads us in triumphal procession in Christ and through us spreads everywhere the fragrance of the knowledge of him. For we are to God the aroma of Christ among those who are being saved and those who are perishing" (2 Corinthians 2:14-15).

I wonder how many times, up on those rocks, cedars have offered rest to exhausted, sun-scorched sojourners? I can imagine with their height and width that they offer great shade—perhaps a canopy of protection for refuge and rest. If I am like a cedar of Lebanon, I too have been called to offer comfort and protection to those who cross my path in need of refuge and shade. I stand on rock, after all. In victory I belong to Christ and cannot be destroyed, so I am to be a safe place. Doesn't this match our calling?

Scripture doesn't offer us descriptions of what we are to become so that we can enjoy some pretty imagery but so that we can be encouraged with a deep understanding of what He has willed and is carrying out in us. See, there are two ways to look at everything. Yes, He is our shade and safe place, but He also has asked us to reflect Him by being the same for others. We can offer shade and safety in this life to those who desperately need it. We are blessed to have faith in Him, and we are asked to reveal our faith to others. He encourages us through Scripture to come to Him in prayer to seek His will and also to pray His will for others. He shows that we can seek healing but that we also can offer healing in His power. We can seek wisdom and impart wisdom.

There are many one-way, self-proclaimed Christians in this world. They are seeking but not offering, asking but not giving. Similarly, some of us may be trying to run around and save the world ourselves without growing deeper and wider. But if we are not deeply rooted or radically transforming into His likeness, we can be blown over by a gentle wind. The holy, inspired Word of God has intentionally compared His children to the beautiful, fragrant, protective, expansive, and nearly indestructible cedar trees that decorate the rocky mountainsides of Lebanon. And He desires for us to see the significance of how, through Him, we are structured to stand strong and stand out, righteous through Him.

Friends, cedars do not grow into their stature and strength overnight. First they must grow deep, very deep. It is not until they take root that they begin to gain in height. The span of their width takes years and years. It is a slow process. They must grow deep before they can grow tall, and at long last they grow wide. Our growth to maturity should look much the same. This "becoming" is not a race or a contest. If He has called you to this mission, you *will* become like a cedar of Lebanon in Psalm 92. You will grow deep and up and out in order to carry out the work that He has designed just for you. "For we are God's workmanship, created in Christ Jesus to do good works which God prepared in advance for us to do" (Ephesians 2:10).

In growing deep, may we reach the spring of life that leads us to His wisdom. In growing tall, may we be sure and confident in who He is and that He is in us. May we always point to Him. In growing wide, may we be a source of shade and hope to those who are hurting and alone. And through it all, may we be a fragrant offering of His love.

> *Lord of all, please strengthen us and root us deep in You. My prayer is that we will be steadfast in our becoming like a cedar of Lebanon, that we will embrace every aspect of depth, width, strength, shade, and height for Your glory, and that we will know in every moment that our foundation cannot be shaken. Grow us up, Lord. Grow us deep, and grow us strong. In Your precious name, Jesus. Amen.*

Weeds

Weeds, if ignored, can cause massive damage to your garden. They are from the dark side, like evil lurking. If you do not regularly and actively pull out weeds from among your vegetables or your flowers, they will encroach upon, squeeze out, and strangle what was intended for beauty and nourishment. Even if they do not manage to kill your plants, at the very least they will make your garden look awful. Trust me, I know this truth intimately. Weeding is just one of those necessary exercises.

In our lives are many things that threaten us like weeds threaten gardens. You and I are like flowers planted by the God of the universe. At various times our emerging blossom are trampled by a reckless person. Sometimes we are strangled by the demands of others. Other times we are taken over and crowded out. We must be active and intentional about removing the weeds in our life so that we may have room to grow. We need to recognize and confess what is not good for us, what hinders our growth and our beauty in Christ. We need to be willing to eliminate what is unhealthy.

Flowers will grow only where I plant them and only if I intentionally take care of them with water and some fertilizer. But weeds—they will grow regardless of what I do. I don't plant them. They just show up. I have to work pretty hard at designing a pleasing landscape, and then I have to wait. Weeds intrude, and they often do so overnight. They don't just show up once a week; they show up every single day. It always turns out best if I work in my garden for a few minutes each morning or afternoon. When addressed early, weeds can be eliminated fairly easily. But if I ignore them for even a few days, they can begin to be rooted in together with what is beautiful. This compromises the health of what promised to be a beautiful bloom, and at that point it may not bloom at all. The weeds will have won, and I will have to start over. But praise the Lord for new starts. New dawns. New days.

We all have weeds in our lives. We are all affected by unhealthy elements that threaten our roots and keep us from becoming who God intends us to be. Weeds take various forms in our lives and are called by different names. Some of these forms are addiction, abuse, greed, vanity, conceit, anger, bitterness, rage, malice, sexual immorality, codependency, insecurity, pride, selfishness, love of money, materialism, position, control, fear, and love of evil (anything that doesn't align with the will of God). These weeds have the potential to strangle us and keep us from growing. So when we realize we have been hindered by weeds, we need to make it a priority to eliminate them and protect ourselves against them. This is an incredible challenge but so very necessary and so deeply beneficial.

As a believer and a child of God on this journey, I admit it is difficult and risky to advise in the area of weeds—that is, sin. No two gardens are exactly alike. Soils have different levels of richness and elements. No two people are the same or are the experiences we go through. For example, a friend of mine and I have both encountered challenges in our marriages. Our marriage struggles share some eerie similarities. My husband and I have a continuing struggle in our relationship. Our connection has been bruised, and we continue to struggle to get it back. My friend divorced her husband. Just because our struggles were similar doesn't mean that the cause was or that the outcome must be. My friend may believe that she can diagnose the cause of the fractures in my marriage because she endured fracture in hers. She may recognize our brokenness, but this does not mean she knows the formula for repair or can determine that it is not fixable.

I use this real example to express how much I do not want to offer "advice" here. There is not a one-size-fits-all solution for weeding out what is unhealthy. Do addicts need to quit? Certainly. But the methods and time required to heal from addiction are not the same for all. All I know for sure is that one can find the strength *and power* through Christ to move forward and make progress. Do unhealthy relationships need to be let go? Possibly yes, but not always. Maybe new boundaries need to be drawn in some cases, but in other cases good-byes are in order. It isn't all black and white, so let's not pretend it is, whether we are seeking to weed out our own inhibitors to growth or we are counseling someone else. Let us be careful not to give stumbling advice. We should always seek the counsel of the Spirit through prayer and fasting.

There are countless things that can inhibit our growth in Christ. Scripture tells us that evil still has power over the world and that Satan wants to destroy our testimonies. That snake is going to introduce weeds into our lives and loves, and many of those weeds might actually look like flowers and fool us at first. We need to be alert. This needs to matter a great deal to us so that we can seek the godly wisdom to recognize and discern what is good and from Him rather than what is not good and therefore not from Him.

So, instead of offering advice, God has prompted me to share some of my own weeds with you. I was a little afraid of this. Weeds, of course, are areas of sin—some known and some we fail to recognize at first. I'll start by sharing some areas of sin that God's Spirit awakened me to and has addressed in my heart. These personal "weeds" that I share are things that needed to be removed from my life so that I could grow deeper into a relationship with Christ. Unlike obvious sin, such as infidelity or criminal activity, I am addressing what was difficult for me to detect, what was less obvious. I share them with you in the hopes that you may also begin to detect where your more subtle "weeds" grow. (I've had some obvious weeds, too, for certain.)

Areas of sin that we do not even recognize as sin can be some of the most powerful strangling weeds. For example, we might not be quick to recognize that some friendships can be tangled in sin. I didn't used to think that the relationship I had with my best friend was sinful in any manner. I adored her and trusted her. We were "besties," but over time I began to realize that I idolized her. In hindsight, now it is very clear to me. I was sinning in my attempt to please her instead of God.

This is an over-simplified explanation, but with her I was "of the world." It wasn't a relationship that honored God in any way, because typically with her I behaved as though He didn't matter. It wasn't sexual sin, substance abuse, or criminal, but it was sin. It was unhealthy. I was tangled in weeds that were strangling out the beauty of heart and spirit that He designed for me and for her. He has since replaced any need that I have to identify a "best friend," and by His Spirit I have been paired with some incredible friends whose hearts are postured toward Him and are healthy toward me and vice versa. I have friendships where we can love Him together and grow in faith together and encourage one another as He has instructed. I also have friendships with people of different beliefs but am able to manage the relationships in ways that honor Him. I do not waiver in who I am, in who He is to me in my life, and in what matters most: His glory.

Many other patches of weeds in my life have been removed by His grace and guidance. Years ago I had a fondness for weekly celebrity gossip magazines. I worked in a doctor's office for a few years. Waiting rooms are notorious for being filled with gossip and fashion magazines. The staff would read them first and then place them in the lobby for patients. I really looked forward to the weekly mail delivery and became mildly addicted to staying on top of what was taking place in certain celebrities' lives. I was fascinated with their lifestyles, homes, vacation spots, and children. I scrutinized their appearance, paying close attention to what they wore to award shows and to the captivating paparazzi images of them going in and out of shopping establishments. I especially enjoyed the scandals, which have a way of making us nonfamous folk feel pretty good about ourselves. Sad but true.

So, the celebrity and gossip mags became a weed in my life. I cared about and focused too much attention on them. Innocent at first, this weed began to take over and strangle a bud that had been trying to blossom. How could I grow in maturity and serve the kingdom if I was focusing my cares on celebrity gossip? Eventually my spirit was convicted that the magazines were feeding a variety of poison into my heart—my heart that was struggling to fight for purity. These seemingly harmless "entertainment" magazines were actually damaging me, by feeding my insecurities and fueling the fires of jealousy, greed, and discontentment. They played a significant part in bending me toward money and "stuff" and in distorting my understanding of beauty and success.

When I realized that for me this was an area of sin, I knew the only way for me to eradicate the negative messages filling me up was to lay it down cold turkey. This particular weed was crowding out my sense of worth in Christ, and it was strangling the root of the blossom I could be. It was difficult; as silly as it may seem, I dealt with some withdrawals. The fact was that I still cared, I still wanted to know, and I still had access. Choosing to stay away from things that are tempting and negative isn't as easy as it seems . We have to pray like crazy for God to release us from the temptations to sin. But we can do it. We can make the decision to look away, and He absolutely can heal us of sinful desires.

These days I have trouble identifying newer celebrities. I joke all the time that if this celebrity or that celebrity delivered me a pizza, I wouldn't have a clue. I wonder how many of us are negatively impacted by what we think we know about the lives of these people we haven't ever met. Not everyone needs to be convicted here, but I sure was. Removing that weed from my life has been an entirely positive thing.

Another weed, for me, was secular music with sexual undertones. Let's face it; some songs are blatantly sexual. I grew up in a musical family and have rhythm in my bones. I was born a dancer and spent a great deal of time in dance clubs in my twenties. Much of that music still makes me move. Music is a great source of enjoyment for me, and I still enjoy an incredible rhythm. And I'll be honest, I can still bust a move. (Yo!)

The problem is that a powerful spiritual conviction came over me with regard to lyrics. The rhythm might move me, but if the lyrics of a song are in opposition to what glorifies God, I am not supposed to listen. You can imagine that under these circumstances I have to turn off the radio—a lot. The battle that rages in my mind is that much of popular music steers my thoughts toward impurity. Sometimes the lyrics even lead me to *desire* impurity. I'm reminded of the power I once had on a dance floor to attract attention. Some pieces of those memories still seem enticing and alluring.

I began to recognize this effect on me as a weed, and I had to take measures to remove it from my life. These days I rarely listen to secular music. Oh, I find some of it, and I have been known to shake my groove thing with my children in our kitchen. But I am desperately careful to invite in only what doesn't harm my mind and what won't damage the hearts of my children. Secular music isn't a weed for everyone, but it has been for me. I share this with you to help you recognize that there may be something seemingly simple and harmless in your life that is in fact a weed threatening what might otherwise dare to bloom. Praise the Lord for inspiring, beautiful, and fun music that shares His powerful message.

I love "love stories." I'm a sucker for the chick flick with a happy ending, but I have begun to see this as a weed in my life as well. Why? Because every time I see the story of happily-ever-after, complete with a gorgeous sunset or an orchard in full bloom, my mind gets hung up on how my marriage is not what chick flicks are made of. I can't even begin to stress how damaging this is to me. If I fantasize that life would be better if I moved to Italy and restored an old dilapidated villa, because a hunk of a man would paint the walls and offer me love till death we do part—well, I have a problem. I know I do. Nothing can make me feel worse about my marriage than a good ole chick flick. On the car ride home from the movie theater, I tend to start tallying in my mind the cons of my marriage relationship. In doing so, I've just been had by a scheme of the devil, and he gained in the grip of the stronghold he has on me.

For me, happily-ever-after love stories do not belong in my life. Not as long as I allow them to hurt my heart. Until I can enjoy love stories for their entertainment value alone without damaging myself with comparisons, I need to refrain. I cannot afford to subscribe to that which isn't reality. You too? I bet a lot of us fall down in this area.

Television is also one of my weeds. Let me confess first that I have not given it up entirely. There is so much garbage on TV these days, but by God's grace I have managed to eliminate most of it from my daily routine. I watch the local and national nightly news, and there are a couple of shows, both comedy and drama, that I regularly watch. But I am careful to explore in my heart what they do for me. Do they make me feel bad about myself or my life? Do they make me wish my life were different? Do they lead me to actions that do not glorify God?

I try to be careful to choose only programming that entertains me and in some aspect either increases my knowledge or compassion. This weed removal was important to me because my previous attitude toward television was unhealthy and damaging to me in countless ways. There are so many positive things that can be exchanged for time spent watching the tube. Today we are taunted by many distractions. Many technologies are alluring and captivating, leading us off the path to righteous living. The greatest time wasters and purpose stealers in my opinion are television and Internet. I realize this may sound overzealous, but I believe that our addictions to technology and media are distractions that hold us back from being who God has created us to be. When we begin to recognize weeds that threaten to strangle our potential, we become intentional about eliminating them by the root and forging better habits.

I hope that we can all be blessed to recognize that weeds inhibit our growth. And we are not alone in this. His Spirit within us helps us do this work of eradicating the sin and the strongholds and helps us to recognize the things we idolize and the activities that lead us to temptation. May we all begin to recognize what needs to go or to be modified in our own lives. May our buds be liberated to bloom.

I mentioned earlier that there are some weeds that look like flowers. If you've spent any time in a flower garden, this may already be ringing true for you. Sometimes you'll see a little colorful bud, and you'll fail to eliminate it because you expect it is going to grow and bloom—that it is meant to be there and that its presence is "good." Some weeds look good and smell good, so we mistake them for good things.

Don't be hard on yourself if it takes you a while to distinguish weeds from flowers. It happens to all of us. And the opposite can be true: we might mistake a flower for a weed and inadvertently get rid of something that was meaningful. I once weeded a coneflower because I confused it for a weed. It was ugly, after all. I looked at it more than once and questioned whether it was a weed or a flower, and I wasn't certain. My mom, more experienced in gardening, inspected the questionable stalk for a moment and was convinced it was a weed, so I yanked it out. A month or so later, I realize that a gorgeous orange coneflower had been in that very bald spot the year before. Doggone it! I had removed something gorgeous and good! I had been a little too quick to judge.

From this experience, I learned that some things are worth keeping and exploring, even if at first they don't match up to our ideals. If you are not sure about a situation or an opportunity, give it a little more thought and prayer rather than hastily determining it to be bad. In my coneflower situation, I even sought advice and wisdom from someone with more knowledge, but I still made the wrong choice. This can happen in serious life decisions as easily as it can happen in a flower garden—in fact, it most likely will at some point. The glory in it for me was that I was able to purchase another flower to plant there. It is now beautiful, and it flourishes.

Bald spot no more. I don't have to mourn what could have been, because I was given another chance to have a beautiful flower garden.

We are given multiple chances to be beautiful blooms. His mercies are new every morning; His grace is enough, and each of us was planted (sown) for such a time as this. He is the master gardener, and together we are His prized bouquet. He will tend to us and protect us from weeds that choke when we seek Him. May we always seek Him. In this we cannot go wrong. We are growing to the heavenlies.

Sweet Father, I am humbled before You for all the ways You are willing to tend to us and protect us; that You only take away what you are willing to replace. Help us to see the less obvious threats against our spirits. Please weed out the inhibitors and help us flourish in your light. In the glorious name of Jesus, amen.

CHAPTER 6

YOUR GARDENER

C

Can I be honest with you about the previous section on weeds? I'm so glad it's over! I'm aware that so many of us are fragile and sensitive about sin, and the last thing I'd want to do is stir up guilt, hopelessness, or doubt. God absolutely adores you and me, so I encourage each of us to not feel discouraged. Jesus said, "I have told you these things, so that in me you may have peace. In this world you will have trouble. But take heart! I have overcome the world" (John 16:33). He is our salvation from the weeds (that is sin) that threaten our purpose.

The power of sin in our lives and in the world is exactly why we need Jesus. He is the Savior. He is the healer of brokenness and the remedy for all that is sick and dying. And He is the ultimate gardener, tending to our weeds. When our faith is placed in His power, we bloom. See, there are areas of sin in our lives that He will awaken us to and that He will give us strength to overcome. There is surely some accountability on our part, but He is very much at work in us. In Him all things are possible.

When I plant a flower in my garden, I do not expect that flower to be the remover of the weeds surrounding it. I, as the gardener, am to be the remover of the weeds. God, as the Father, is the Healer of our sin. He isn't handing you a checklist and then stopping by to check in on you once in a while. By His Spirit, He is dwelling *right* inside of you. He is present in your heart and mind, and He is your strength. And He is *not waiting* for your sins to be gone before He can use you to serve Him. Our sin will never be completely gone.

Remember, we cannot reflect a crystal-clear image of Christ in the mirror and out into the world. At best we will reflect a vague image. But our sin doesn't keep God from loving us. Only lack of faith (belief) can separate us from Him. As Paul tells us, "Without faith it is impossible to please God, because anyone who comes to him must believe that he exists and that He rewards those who earnestly seek him" (Hebrews 11:6). With faith we must seek to find Him in the midst of our sin. He will see to it that we grow among the weeds and that over time the weeds will become fewer and less threatening.

He will even use the experiences of our sin as a platform to bless others. Yes, He uses our messes to share His message of redemption with others. To be a blessing to others, we must serve. *Share heart.* He has begun a work in us and will not cease until we are complete: "being confident in this, that he who began a good work in you will carry it on to completion until the day of Christ Jesus" (Philippians 1:6).

Rest in this: we are just the bloom. He is the gardener. He will cultivate, nourish, water, prune, trim, sow, and weed us. With Him in control of gardening us, maturity, vibrancy, and bursts of beauty are inevitable. He just asks that we seek Him. Seek and ye shall find. Knock and He will answer. There isn't a whisper of His name that He fails to hear and answer to.

"Ask and it will be given to you; seek and you will find; knock and the door will be opened to you."
Matthew 7:7

❧

Fruit and Faith

Abraham believed. He had faith, and his faith was credited to him as righteousness, as we are taught in Genesis 15:6. Faith is many things but it is not scientific. It is heart. It is hope and belief and trust. Whoever believes in Jesus will have eternal life, we are taught in John 3:16. We can recognize true believers by the "fruit" they produce, according to John 15. Faith without deeds is dead, according to James 2:26. Scripture points to these truths over and over. We are saved by grace through faith, not by works, as Paul's letter to the Ephesians states (2:8). What I have accepted from all of this is that sincere faith inspires action—action to move others to faith. Whether your fruit tree produces a bushel or a peck, every apple matters.

"Thus, by their fruit you will recognize them." (Matthew 7:20)

"This is to my Father's glory, *that you bear much fruit, showing yourselves to be my disciples.* As the Father has loved me, so have I loved you. Now remain in my love. If you obey my commands, you will remain in my love, just as I have obeyed my Father's commands and remain in his love. I have told you this so that my joy may be in you and that your joy may be complete. My command is this: Love each other as I have loved you. Greater love has no one than this, that he lay down his life for his friends." (John 15:8-13, emphasis added)

"So I say, live by the Spirit, and you will not gratify the desires of the sinful nature. For the sinful nature desires what is contrary to the Spirit, and the Spirit what is contrary to the sinful nature. They are in conflict with each other, so that you do not do what you want. But if you are led by the Spirit, you are not under law. The acts of the sinful nature are obvious: sexual immorality, impurity and debauchery; idolatry and witchcraft; hatred, discord, jealousy, fits of rage, selfish ambition, dissensions, factions and envy; drunkenness, orgies, and the like. I warn you, as I did before, that those who live like this will not inherit the kingdom of God. But the *fruit of the Spirit* is love, joy, peace, patience, kindness, goodness, faithfulness, gentleness and self-control. Against such things there is no law. Those who belong to Christ Jesus have crucified the sinful nature with its passions and desires. Since we live by the Spirit, let us keep in step with the Spirit. Let us not become conceited, provoking and envying each other." (Galatians 5:16-26, emphasis added)

Do you recall that the cedars in Lebanon were declared to bear fruit in old age and that we would be like them? Fruit is sweet and nourishing. For us to be bearers of fruit means that we will be producers of what the Spirit teaches us and freely gives us. Every one of us is a seed God has sown into this world. And He has made us to be fruitful. We are to produce something for Him; something that points to His sovereignty and His majesty.

As our own seed matures into fruit, we are to sow seeds too. This cycle is made possible by the Spirit—that we bear fruit and sow seeds. Believing isn't fruit, though it leads to the production of fruit. Going to church isn't fruit, but it can lead to knowledge and wisdom; it can increase faith and aid in fruit production. Fruit isn't produced by our actions. It is produced in our hearts and our convictions that lead to action. Love is fruit. Paul wrote, "The entire law is summed up in a single command: Love your neighbor as yourself" (Galatians 5:14). Everything done in love for the kingdom is fruit. So we are called to be fruitful—not *just* to grow but to grow and produce something that the world can taste, see, and smell— and enjoy and share. Fruit is produced by us through the Spirit—His Holy Spirit that He sent to dwell within us. He doesn't want us to miss this. We have to move beyond belief.

JOURNAL ENTRY

~ THE TURTLE IN MY REARVIEW ~

There are two route choices for me to travel to and from the sticks and bricks that I call home. One is the ever-hurried interstate; the other is the peaceful, lush, scenic back roads. I drive the back roads as much as possible. The view of the river impresses my eyes every time. The forest of trees and the forced slow weave back and forth of twists and turns do what I need; they slow me down.

Sometimes I see spectacular, mysterious birds hanging out in the river water. They look like cranes. Tall, lanky birds standing still like statues. They disappear into the landscape with their magical camouflage trickery. But I know they are there, so I scan the waterscape until I find them. They make me smile. I make them smile too, I imagine.

Occasionally I see a turtle crossing the road. Most of the time I pull over like a taxi driver and load it in to drop it off at the next water spot. I mean, why not? Turtles are slow, and cars are fast. You do the math.

Today I passed a turtle in the road. He was quite large. Honestly, I was afraid of him, too intimidated to offer him a ride. So instead I passed him by and then watched him in my rearview. He was ambitiously bookin' it, and I'll be honest, I was cheering him on: "GO, TURTLE, GO!" I did not want the aforementioned mathematical equation to shatter his shell and destroy his life.

As I watched him trek on to a safer place, and as he became smaller and smaller from my vantage point, I realized, aren't I just like a turtle?

• I am always aiming for a better place but not always getting there.

- Sometimes I am safe. Sometimes helpless.
- Sometimes I am too dang slow.
- Sometimes I really need to be carried.
- I am often alone.
- I never know what is up ahead.
- Most people pass on by. Very few stay and help out.
- I am incredibly thirsty, always in search of a saving drink.
- Sometimes I bite, and scare people.
- I can carry a hard outer shell.
- Someone is usually watching me in the rearview.

Turtles do not give up. They are always in search of a nourishing source. Though slow, they move. They go.

As long as my heart is beating I hope I never stop moving with purpose, like a turtle.

PART III

You and me: works in progress.

All of our days.

May we be blessed with an inner eye to see ourselves the way our heavenly Father does, a one-of-a-kind masterpiece in the making. He is the potter. We are the clay from mud, moistened and squeezed, stretched and balled up, pressed in and opened, formed by His hand and preserved for all eternity.

CHAPTER 7

A BEAUTIFUL YOU

vintage heart

The first time I can recall hearing the word *vintage* was in my early twenties. Some clothiers had popped up in town touting vintage clothing. Everything was unique, slightly worn, from a previous time. Only certain people could really pull it off from a style perspective. I wasn't one of those people. Instead of the clothing making me look cool and interesting, I made it look awkward. No matter how much I wanted it to be, vintage just wasn't for me.

These days, vintage is in again. Many of us drool over just about anything vintage, from cars and jewelry to clothing and furniture. I am particularly fond of old, worn pieces of painted furniture. By watching my mom, I learned quite a bit about the process of refinishing furniture. There are many detailed steps to the process. First, the old has to be removed. You begin by coating the wood with a stripping chemical and then scrape off the old paint with a dulled tool and steel wool. This stripping and scraping step might have to be repeated several times to get all the old finish off. Then you sand and smooth the wood in preparation for the new finish. Finally, after the new finish is applied and dried, it is best to seal it with wax. Of course, depending on the finish, several other techniques may be added to achieve a particular look. But the result is to either make something old look new again or to make something old look much cleaner, more beautiful, and ready to be useful once again.

A wayward sinner is restored to God through salvation in much the same way. I suppose by the time Jesus snatched a hold of me I had been roughed up and worn out. Not a prized vintage piece but a ragged, shabby hunk of junk. Really. I deeply desire to be a prized vintage treasure, beautiful and useful again.

Consider these definitions.

Vintage— *denoting something of high quality, especially something from the past or characteristic of the best period of a person's work.*
Shabby—*in poor condition through long and hard use or lack of care.*
Restoration—*the process of repairing or renovating; as to restore something to its original condition.*

What if we were to recognize and believe in the promise that we can be spiffed up and fully restored? What if we were to boldly believe that God is the restorer of shattered hearts? What if our hearts could recover from the long and hard use or lack of care? What if they could again reflect what characterizes the very best period of the love we've shared? I bet we'd all be willing to pay high dollar for that. We'd all have vintage hearts.

The Lord God of all creation began the restoration of our fractured hearts when we met with Him at the cross. He gave a song to David, and we can sing it too: "Create in me a clean heart, O Lord, and renew a right spirit within me" (Psalm 51:10). David was a man after God's own heart, and yet he had the sense to know when his heart was in a shabby state. He knew that only the Lord of all could restore his heart back to the characteristic of his better days. He knew that being indwelled by the Spirit would restore him and renew him and that he could live as a masterpiece. We have been broken, but by His hand we are being restored so that we each have a vintage heart. *Now, that deal ain't too shabby.*

JOURNAL ENTRY

~ IN THE SPIRIT ~

Many Christians whisper when they speak of the Holy Spirit—or worse, they utter not a word. The Holy Spirit is our most treasured gift this side of heaven. To think that God would give us a portion of His very Spirit in our heart and mind when we acknowledge Him…I just don't know how not to get excited about that. His Spirit encourages and guides our heart and mind. The Spirit is our counsel, our nudge and push, the fibers of faith, our loving conviction. The Spirit is ours to be led by. The Spirit within you is like a tiny fragment of sharing a mind and heart with Christ. Scripture says it is an early deposit on our future inheritance: "Now it is God who makes both us and you stand firm in Christ. He anointed us, set his seal of ownership on us, and put his Spirit in our hearts as a deposit, guaranteeing what is to come" (2 Corinthians 1:21-22). And "you were also included in Christ when you heard the word of truth, the gospel of your salvation. Having believed, you were marked in him with a seal, the promised Holy Spirit, who is a deposit guaranteeing our inheritance until the redemption of those who are God's possession—to the praise of his glory" (Ephesians 1:13-14).

When I look up *Spirit* in the index of my *Quest Study Bible* or on BibleGateway.com, the list of references is exhausting. Joyfully exhausting. This is the holiness of Christ, always accessible and always helpful. Truly, the Christian journey cannot be authentically walked without the Holy Spirit. He is not a dismissible third of the Trinity. The Spirit is God, fully alive within. Jesus said,

> "If you love me, you will obey what I command. And I will ask the Father, and he will give you another Coun-

selor to be with you forever—the Spirit of truth."
(John 14:15-17)

"All this I have spoken while still with you. But the
Counselor, the Holy Spirit, whom the Father will send
in my name, will teach you all things and will remind
you of everything I have said to you." (John 14:25-26)

The truth that is resting within me is that we not only can live this
life *for* God, but we can live it *with* Him. That blesses my soul and
encourages me to walk on. God is *with us* at all times. He doesn't
come and go. He stays. He will never abandon our hearts. We may
ignore Him or refuse to seek and obey Him, or we may fail to
believe it, but He is with us. The more we seek Him, the more His
presence is known and felt. Persistence in faith makes His movement indisputable.

`Ripe

My heart has been seeking the words to express what the Spirit has
taught me in my believing years so far. This fragile thumping thing inside
me, pumping the blood through and through, also wants to expose His
heart for you. My God (as in OMG), He loves you so much. But really,
what good is the who, what, when, where, and why if there isn't at least a
hint to the how?

A flower doesn't have to be told how to grow. A piece of fruit doesn't
have to study how to ripen. God takes care of every piece of that. His
power is at work at all times, coming in from every location and accom-
plishing every good thing. A peach tree is going to bear fruit, and those

peaches will ripen. (And I might add, when washed, sliced and served in a bowl of cream, those peaches will magnificently glorify God. *Amen?!*)

But may we see this: before that wonderful fruit ripens, it is hard and bitter. When it ripens too much, fruit is soft and flavorless. There is absolutely a perfect stage of ripeness for harvest. I believe that you and I are ripe right now. We are sweet, no longer bitter. We are flavorful, and we will not ever be overripe. Our sweetness can last and last and last throughout the rest of our lives and beyond.

We are also the seeds that He has sown, tended, and is harvesting now. We are the thing that He has intended for beauty, and He will see to it that we are fruitful. Let us know that we are ripe—right now. Consider this defnition of *"Ripe"* ~ developed to the point of readiness for harvesting; fully matured; rich and intense. *"Ripe for"* means ~ arrived at the fitting stage or time for a particular action or purpose. Oh, precious ones, we are *ripe* and we are *ripe for*. He created us for such a time as this. Let us harvest this sweetness from His garden like a heavenly scented remembrance that will never wither away. And may we live radiantly, intentionally, purposefully, and eternally!

R = Radiant. May we shine and glow His radiance into the world.

I = Intentional. May we intentionally love with the hope that is His.

P = Purposeful. May we know that He purposed us for such a time as this.

E = Eternal. May we set our eyes on eternity, the kingdom of heaven.

LEAN ~ STRETCH ~ ROTATE ~ GROW

For Mother's day, my then four-year-old son's classroom decorated tiny flowerpots, and with my precious flowerpot I was given a bag of seed. Sweet. It took me about a week to get around to the dirty little project. I filled the small flowerpot, delicately decorated with haphazard brush strokes of paint, and painted buttons glued around the rim, with potting soil. I dropped in the seed and added water.

Things began to grow. Such is the case with seed that is sown, watered, and nourished.

As it sits in the kitchen window, I see my sweet little flowerpot several times a day. It truly begs to be repotted into a larger pot now, but then it would no longer fit perfectly in the window. It craves the sun. It leans and stretches toward the nourishment of the sun's rays. Occasionally I have to rotate the plant because too much leaning and stretching in one direction makes it lopsided.

A child of God is truly the same. I am a planted, nurtured, and nourished seed. I am leaning toward the Son of Man, stretching out to reach His powerful, healing robe, longing to bloom into His likeness and turning in every direction to see and share His beauty.

Lean. Stretch. Rotate. Grow.

I'm a dirty little project, but He continues to nurture me and always gives me what I need, when I need it.

CHAPTER 8

LEAN

"Trust in the Lord with all your heart and lean not on your own understanding. In all your ways acknowledge Him and He will make your paths straight."

Proverbs 3:5-6

When I think of "lean," many images come to mind. I think of lean meat that has been rid of excess fat. A lot of what we do in our lives can be classified as "excess." We not only eat too much, we also worry too much, want too much, have too much, spend too much, and waste too much time thinking of ourselves—and only ourselves. Sure, we think about our kids and our friends, but they are all still just extensions of "us." How often do we spend time thinking of our neighbors and their kids or the orphans in Haiti or the prisoners on death row or the needs of the elderly or the poor? Many of us do not spend much time thinking about things, people, or places that have nothing to do with us. Instead, we think too much of ourselves. Our minds and hearts could be leaner. We could stand to trim the fat and spend time chewing on (and really digesting) more of the things that God cares about.

The term *lean* also conjures up the image of a physically fit person— a person who has worked hard to obtain that shape, that physique, that appearance, that size, that ability, that strength, or that endurance. Those things require focus and determination, drive and commitment, time and desire. A person of faith should be this dedicated to the practice of leaning on God. Could you just imagine the spiritual strength and power?

I'm not so great at standing for long periods of time. Occasionally I need to sit, but in many circumstances there may not be a seat available. In those times I might search for a wall to lean against. I, like you, from time to time need a place to rest my weight against something strong enough to hold me up and take the pressure off the places that are growing weak, like my ankles, knees, back, and neck. I can stand upright on my own only for so long before it all just starts to hurt.

When I visualize a weary person tired of standing on his or her own two feet, leaning into a wall, it reminds me that the Lord God is a pillar of strength. He intends for us to lean on Him. He is the solid Father who will never let us fall, nor will he ever refuse to carry all the weight we possess. We can only lean on things that will hold us steady—solid strength we can trust. God's Word shows us we can lean on Him. He can manage our weight and our weaknesses. He can hold us forever. Leaning on God means having faith in Him through His son Jesus and trusting in His ways rather than our own.

I have been guilty of placing my trust in a friend, relying on that person for my joy and my hope, my fun, and all my tomorrows. I have been guilty of placing my faith in family, expecting them to come through in every situation, whether it be encouragement or empowerment. I have placed my faith in my children, believing that they could be my source for fulfilling every dream. I have placed my faith in the love of a significant other, expecting and believing that he could protect my heart forever and keep it safe from damage. Instead I have faced devastation and hopelessness. I have been left spinning, dazed and confused. I have been sucked into sinking sand and left nearly breathless. This is simply what happens when faith isn't built on a solid, unbreakable foundation. Are we still leaning into our own understanding?

He will carry nothing of us if we do not lean on Him in faith. No matter what we might be lifting, if we do not lean into Him, He will allow us to carry our weight alone, and it will weigh us down into the ground, literally. Nothing but the solid rock of salvation (requiring faith) can hold us up.

❧

How Do You Lean Into God?

"He guides the humble in what is right and teaches them his way."
Psalm 25:9

I believe the act of leaning on God, "pressing in," requires humility first. A proud person will not surrender easily, and we are all guilty of being prideful. To be humble before God is to acknowledge that He, as God of the universe, is in charge—and you are not. That's tough. Not everyone is willing to humble himself. Not everyone is willing to surrender.

If you have never experienced a loss or a failure, you may not recognize a need to surrender. If your life is going great, you may have a high level of pride standing in your way toward humility. You might be sitting on top of the world. Prideful people (all of us at some point) should heed the warning in Proverbs 16:18-19: "Pride goes before destruction, a haughty spirit before a fall. Better to be lowly in spirit and among the oppressed than to share plunder with the proud." Pride leads to destruction, while humility spares us from it. If you believe in a supernatural God but are not being pulled by spiritual forces to your knees or you do not feel a desperate need to serve Him for His reasons and purposes, you may be facing an utter devastation in some area of your life. Don't wait to be forced to your knees. Go now in surrender.

James wrote, "Submit yourselves, then, to God. Resist the devil, and he will flee from you. Come near to God and he will come near to you.

Wash your hands, you sinners, and purify your hearts, you double-minded. Grieve, mourn and wail. Change your laughter to mourning and your joy to gloom. Humble yourselves before the Lord, and he will lift you up" (James 4:7-10). Wow! He does not exactly beat around the bush, does he?

It is believed that the James that wrote these verses was the half-brother of Jesus. He was writing to warn the believers of those days that they were falling headfirst into some bad habits. Perhaps they were boastful and proud? Maybe they were too comfortable in life? Maybe James was reminding them that their salvation was not just a moment of acceptance but a commitment to live life for the purpose of glorifying God with their lives.

No matter how good our day may have gone, how successful or happy we are, James doesn't want us to forget that the Lords' heart continues to grieve for our sin, that He cares about injustice, and that He is pursuing the lost sheep (unbelievers) through those of us that He counts among His children. He called us to be His ambassadors, not to just party up our salvation. An ambassador goes out on Christ's behalf to invite others to His well of salvation. An ambassador of Christ represents Him. That is what we are to be and what we are to do.

Peter wrote, "Humble yourselves, therefore, under God's mighty hand, that he may lift you up in due time" (1 Peter 5:6). This verse suggests that the only way up is down. Humility and surrender make room for God to increase your faith and to show up in indisputable ways. How can God show us His power if we are too proud to look for it and too stubborn to see it?

I love word pictures because I best learn with my imagination. This verse in 1 Peter talks about God's mighty hand. If I humble myself under God's mighty hand, I am indeed "under" Him. I imagine the force of a strong man grasping his large palm on the head of a small child and forcing the child's stillness. Sometimes I do this to my children (safely, of course) if I need them to calm down or be still at the grocery store or at a friend's house. The action of placing my hand on their head can't really hold them there; they could escape that if they wanted it to. But instead it sends them a message: "be quiet" or "be still." To humble oneself before God requires both. Be quiet and listen for Him. Be still and let Him do what He has been trying to do all along, to mold you into His likeness.

This verse also suggests that in your humble state, the Lord God will hold you there and will keep you humbled. This is both frightening and refreshing. The humbling process can be painful, in all honesty. It typically strips things that need to be removed from our prideful hearts so that we may grow. Ultimately, this process is refining and redeeming, and we eventually come out better for it. As our pride fades and is replaced by humility, we reflect Christ more vividly. Our humbling seasons may involve the stripping away of possessions, health, relationships, or status, but when we humble ourselves before God, He does so much more to lead us into the design and plan He has for us. It may be difficult to recognize this "stripping down" as a blessing, but it is indeed, and this blessing simply cannot occur without humility. We can humble ourselves before Him, or He will humble us before everyone.

I'm always thankful for a Proverb to cut to the chase. Consider, for instance, Proverbs 11:2: "When pride comes, then comes disgrace, but with humility comes wisdom." And Proverbs 15:33: "The fear of the Lord teaches a man wisdom, and humility comes before honor."

God started teaching me about humility in my childhood. As providence would have it, I auditioned for the class play and was awarded a part. I played the part of "humility." I do not have a single other memory about that play, only that I had no idea what "humility" meant; still I was to embody this characteristic in my performance. My teacher had coached me exactly the way to deliver my lines. I made it through the performance believably by mimicking her tone and expression. Bottom line, my humility was a fraud, an act. Ironically, the true meaning of "humility" wasn't taught to me at that time, though I did pick up on how to "pretend." I might have understood, even at the young age of eight, had examples been used, but humility didn't become a concept that I understood until I was well into my adulthood. (That is a sad confession!)

The necessity of having a character of humility runs as a prominent theme throughout Scripture. To ignore that pride is destructive and humility is necessary to serve and honor God is equivalent to elevating yourself above Him. No one has a better plan than God. No one has more wisdom than God. No one has more time than God. We don't even come close. We have to get that to get Him. We have to get that to get to heaven.

Proverbs 11:2 says, "When pride comes, then comes disgrace, but with humility comes wisdom." This proverb teaches us that a prideful person will experience disgrace. It is inevitable. However, a humble person will be blessed with wisdom. Wisdom in Christ cannot and will not be achieved any other way. Fear of the Lord is reverence and respect for Him. Only the humble can be honored in heaven. This makes me crave humility. I want to be on my knees before our Lord, and I don't mind if my knees sink through the floor as if it were sinking sand. I want to be stripped of pride. I want to be refined. I want to be content to wait until His due time to be lifted up. I just want to be lifted. I don't want to climb.

An entire chapter of Philippians is dedicated to imitating the humility of Christ. Philippians 2:3-4 states, "Do nothing out of selfish ambition or vain conceit, but in humility consider others better than yourselves. Each of you should look not only to your own interests, but also to the interests of others." This is a hard truth—to not ever allow ourselves to be driven and motivated by our own selfish ambitions. Even something as straightforward as a job interview can be plagued with selfish ambition. Did you fluff the resume? Did you exaggerate your accomplishments? It may seem innocent as you are just trying to get a job in this struggling economy, and *you* need a job more than the other thousands of unemployed. *See?* Ouch. Our ambitions may be selfish by default. We may have to choose and even practice refusing to make it "all about me" by laying down our own motives and trusting God with our lives instead.

Humility doesn't rush to beat the other car to the parking space.

Humility doesn't use elbows to force its way to the seat at the concert.

Humility doesn't take the last cookie out of the jar without offering it to someone else.

Humility lets traffic merge.

Humility waits until everyone else has been served.

Humility sponsors a child to go to camp.

Humility doesn't interrupt the other person speaking.

Humility is satisfied at the end of the line.

Humility puts herself in other person's shoes.

Humility cries for injustice of the poor, the orphaned, and the oppressed.

Humility stands up for a cause, for someone else.

Humility does not manipulate outcomes.

Humility could take up a thousand pages of this book.

Peter tells us, "All of you clothe yourselves with humility toward one another because God opposes the proud but shows favor to the humble" (I Peter 5:5). Some translations say to "clothe yourself *in* humility." In other words, wear it like a garment. You wouldn't leave home without your pants. We shouldn't consider rising out of bed in the mornings without first wrapping ourselves in a humble robe.

Authentic faith will lead us to humility.

∽

Lean—As an Act of Love

When you were a child, did you ever lean on your momma or daddy or grandparent and wrap your arms around their legs? Sometimes we can lean on Christ as a show of affection. You can lean on Him out of love, not just out of need. This will have to take whatever form you feel is natural for you. It may be singing to praise Him, or it may be resting in Him, or it may be staying silent and still while meditating on His wonder and His majesty. You can lean on Him with your hope. You can cry out for His mercy. You can seek His wisdom.

One of my favorite pictures of leaning is in the Gospels. During the Last Supper, John leans back on Jesus (see John 21:20). He literally reclines and rests on his friend, our Savior and Lord, Christ Jesus. Jesus offers comfort and rest. Although we cannot physically lean on Him at suppertime, we can place the entire weight of our being, of our lives, our hopes, our sorrows, our journey, and our eternity on Him. We can lean on His faithfulness. In fact, He desires this of us each day.

∾

Lean—As an Act of Faith

Although leaning on the understanding of God rather than on our own understanding requires humility, leaning into the Lord is an act of faith. And what is faith but belief and trust? Belief and trust. Belief. And trust. Trust. Trust certainly doesn't always seem natural at first.

We find this passage in Isaiah:

Do you not know? Have you not heard? The LORD is the everlasting God, the Creator of the ends of the earth. He will not grow tired or weary, and his understanding no one can fathom. He gives strength to the weary, and increases the power of the weak. Even youths grow tired and weary, and young men stumble and fall; but those who hope in the Lord will renew their strength. They will soar on wings like eagles; they will run and not grow weary, they will walk and not faint.

From these verses in Isaiah, I love the phrase "those who hope in the Lord." To hope in the Lord implies we must trust Him, have faith, and patience. Trusting in God requires that we be confident He is faithful. Trust (hope) in the Lord requires that you seek Him, seek His wisdom, seek His truth, seek His love—and not fight against His will. You will not stand in the way of what He is trying to accomplish *in you* or *through you*.

Trust is a heavy word, and for many of us it is intimidating. If you feel called to serve God, you have to trust Him—that is, to rely on His integrity, His power, and His love. This is a nonnegotiable basis of Christianity. If you believe in Him but you do not "trust" in Him, you are saying you don't really "believe" in Him. Or rather you believe in who He is, but not necessarily in what He can do. Or perhaps you think you can design a better outcome if you take matters into your own hands, or you are afraid He might not answer your prayers precisely according to your specifications. For example, perhaps a couple prays for biological children, but God's plan involves adoption instead. An answered prayer…but not *the* answer? Do you trust that God's plan for you is better than your own?

For me, the bottom line about trust, faith, and hope in the Lord is this: He blessed me with this life, so my life belongs to Him. We have a tendency to believe that we are the owners and keepers of our own lives, but we really are not. Your life is His, and it is for Him. God has a kingdom plan and a divine purpose that are bigger than just you (and me). You were created to accomplish your role in His plan and all that you are is for Him. Your relationships are for Him. Your service is for Him. Your career is for Him. Your joy is for Him. Your children are for Him. Your money is for Him. Your hobbies and pastimes are all for Him. He gave you all of this for Him, for His glory and His kingdom.

What you do, the ways you serve, and how you live have direct effects on His heavenly kingdom. He is going to give you many opportunities to advance His kingdom. For you to make the biggest impact on yourself, your family, your friends, neighbors, coworkers, and total strangers passing by in the grocery store, you have to trust Him. You have to trust Him with your skills, your health, your finances, your relationships, and your career. This is no area of your life excused from the "lean" factor. Prop it all up against Him. There is no one else who can fit your life and your purpose in the palm of his hand.

The most unnatural element of trusting God is to be relaxed about it. I'm not sure that the Scriptures specifically say, "Hey, relax!" but they do tell us to rest in Him and not to fear. One reminder of this is in Joshua 1:9: "Have I not commanded you? Be strong and courageous. Do not be afraid; do not be discouraged, for the LORD your God will be with you wherever you go." I believe God knew that trusting Him would be difficult for us because we like to test things first, don't we? When I am hiking and get ready to cross a riverbed, I have to stick my toes in first. And before I will place all my weight on a rock, I try to move it with my feet and apply just a little weight before I trust that it is sturdy enough to keep me safe.

With God, trust is more an act of determination than an experiment. It is a leap, not a timid step. And while that may not seem like something to be relaxed about, He promises peace: "Now may the Lord of peace himself give you peace at all times and in every way. The Lord be with all of you" (2 Thessalonians 3:16). God also uses His Word to encourage us over and over not to fear. We truly are like little children who do not listen and heed advice. We have to be told a thousand times, as in John 14:17, "Peace I leave with you; my peace I give you. I do not give to you as the world gives. Do not let your hearts be troubled and do not be afraid."

And, in the event we need more reminders...

"For I am the LORD your God who takes hold of your right hand and says to you, 'Do not fear. I will help you.'" (Isaiah 41:13)

"The LORD will fight for you; you need only to be still." (Exodus 14:14)

"Be strong and courageous. Do not be afraid or terrified because of them, for the LORD your God goes with you; he will never leave you nor forsake you. ... The LORD himself goes before you and will be with you; he will never leave you nor forsake you. Do not be afraid; do not be discouraged." (Deuteronomy 31:6, 8)

And so we know and rely on the love God has for us. God is love. Whoever lives in love lives in God and God in him. In this way, love is made complete among us so that we will have confidence on the day of judgment, because in this world we are like him. There is no fear in love. But perfect love drives out fear, because fear has to do with punishment. The one who fears is not made perfect in love. (I John 4:16-19)

Leaning into God means trusting Him even with your fears. The fear of failure, the fear of dying, the fear of loneliness, the fear of bankruptcy, the fear of unforgiveness, and all other fears can be surrendered to Christ, who will transform them into hope and love. Give your fears to God, and He will give you comfort and strength. There is no better path than the one He has made ahead of you.

Everything you go through in life can shape you and glorify Him, even illness, loss, and failure. Everything you fear today, if surrendered, can point to His love and His hope. And as much as it is contrary to most of our desires, even death can serve an eternal kingdom purpose for God. Remember, it is all for Him, and He knows what He is doing, though we may not understand the full scope of it in the here and now.

This life just isn't about this life. The eternal life is where we get to experience perfection and never feel sorrow. This life isn't just about *this life*. It is about God's eternal kingdom in heaven, and we have been given faith assignments to live by without fear: Love God. Love others as you love yourself. Fellowship with and encourage other Christians. Share the gospel. Give to the poor. Don't love money. Go fishing for other people. Praise the Lord and confess His name. Confess your sins. Pray. Do your best to reflect Christ to the watching world. Forgive. Be slow to anger. And finally, exercise a faith that isn't fearful. There is simply no room in this gig for fear.

Oh Father, help us begin by giving us strength to lean confidently into you and to forego our own understandings. Increase our faith and intensify our love for you so that we can feel the solid foundation upon which we stand, your precious saving Son. Comfort us as we learn to lean. Remember we feel like we are falling until we find our safety in your hands. Lord, above all, give us the desire to want your ways and the power to abandon our temptation to control. In Jesus, amen.

CHAPTER 9

STRETCH

J ust like the flowerpot in the window whose tiny stalks and petals stretch toward the glorious sunshine, craving to be bathed by its light and nourishment, we too must stretch toward the Son. We will be bathed by His grace, mercy, spiritual gifts, love, and wisdom.

Accepting Christ as your personal Savior is the critical first step. Only then can you lean on His promises and His faithfulness. We cannot lean if we do not believe. But the life lived in the space between believing in God and actually going to be with Him in eternity requires the stretch. This is where we reach out to Christ every day of our lives, in all that we do, in all that we think, and in all that we feel. There will never be a more transforming stretch than reaching out to Christ.

In my mind's eye, I visualize an athlete stretching in an act of preparation for a sport. Whether reaching in the air for the ball, running the race, reaching for a partner in a dance, or bending for a balance beam, there is no sport where stretching isn't critical. No matter what the game, what the sport, or what the physical art, you simply won't be the best you can be if you do not stretch. Whether you're a beginner or a pro, stretching never ceases to be in the equation. In fact, stretching becomes more critical over time, and with age. I believe it is also true that the most unnatural or awkward stretching positions benefit us the most, as with yoga and Pilates. A really good session of stretching can even be painful. My high school track coach used to say, "No pain, no gain." Spiritual stretching may be similar.

My mind's eye also envisions the artist stretching a canvas in preparation for a painting. At first it is a blank canvas that he stretches and smoothes over and over again, working out every little kink. The canvas is eventually adhered to a solid frame that will steadily hold it in place while its creator brings a masterpiece to life with physical strokes, bold texture, and vibrant color. No detail will be left out. If that canvas remains rolled up and unpainted in the corner of the studio, it offers nothing. Unstretched, it is unremarkable.

I imagine a mother reaching her arms out*stretched* for the child getting off the school bus, just to show her protecting love. Her stretch is an action of love that embraces and holds close.

At four foot nine inches small, my mother-in-law must climb on a stool and stretch her entire body, on her tippy toes, to reach something in the upper cabinet over the microwave. If she doesn't extend every extremity *beyond what is normal* for her short body, she'll never reach it.

Stretching involves bending, reaching, and extending.

Bend.

Reach.

Extend.

The sad truth is that many Christians never stretch. They don't reach, bend, or extend. If all we ever do is lean, we fail to move. We fail to put our faith into action. Leaning leads to hope. Stretching is the action that gives it power. Paul wrote, "Everyone who competes in the games goes into strict training. They do it to get a crown that will not last, but we do it to get a crown that will last forever." And "run in such a way as to get the prize" (1 Corinthians 9:25, 24b).

The stretch is both the most intimidating and the most exciting opportunity in living a life intended for Christ Jesus. It is where we make an *intentional* decision to step outside of our comfort zone. It is where we bend to serve the "least of these" (see Matthew 25:40). We reach toward what seems unreachable, and we extend in offering all that God has given us back to Him by serving others.

"But encourage one another daily, as long as it is called today, so that none of you may be hardened by sins deceitfulness."
Hebrews 3:13

"I pray that you may be *active* in sharing your faith, so that you will have a full understanding of every good thing we have in Christ."
Philemon 1:6

Reach for Jesus.

Where You'll Find Him

It is not uncommon for me to receive private messages through social networks from people who observe my blog posts and updates about my faith. Occasionally someone invites me to have coffee and then ask questions such as "How is it that you are able to write about Jesus like you know Him personally?" Or "Where does your faith come from?" I even had one precious woman say to me, "If I thought I could have a real relationship with God I would try, but I don't know if I believe and I wouldn't know how anyway." These questions and comments both horrify me and bless me in ways that words cannot do justice. There are just so many people out there (most of whom are not attending church) who want to find Jesus and get to know Him.

Theologically speaking, Jesus isn't hiding, but for our purposes here I am approaching this as though we are looking for Him. He wants to be found! As I have mentioned already, I spent many years as a "believer," even though I had not been transformed until much later, when my belief became genuine. I now realize that Jesus will not pour into us unless we choose to open up to receive Him. He will not force us to believe, nor will He force us to stretch. In my observation we have to make each choice.

Remember, stretching isn't easy and can be painful. One of my pastors recently journeyed from America to Tanzania to climb Mt. Kilimanjaro. There is no way he would have made it to the summit without stretching, bending, reaching, and extending. In other words, he didn't summit by accident, and neither will you or I. He made the choice to go and to climb with dedication and determination. Like any mountain climber, we also must intentionally reach. When we do, Jesus will respond swiftly to bring us to high places. We'll find Him *there*, in our willingness to receive Him.

The three most common ways I believe that Jesus pours into us (where we will find Him) are through Scripture, prayer, and community. Romans 5:5 says, "And hope does not disappoint us, because God has *poured* out his love into our hearts by the Holy Spirit, whom he has given us" (emphasis added). To receive His pouring, we need to open our hearts through Bible study, regular time in prayer, and committed time in fellowship with other believers in church, community groups, or other settings where believers gather. I know that if I do not participate regularly in these ways, I am not reaching. If I am not reaching, He won't grab my hand and lead me. It's as simple as that.

He Is in the Scriptures

The Bible says that Jesus is the Word made flesh, and "In the beginning was the Word, and the Word was with God, and the Word was God" (John 1:1). And in John 1:14, we learn that "the Word became flesh and made his dwelling among us. We have seen his glory, the glory of the One and Only, who came from the Father, full of grace and truth." Jesus is the words on the pages, and the words on the pages are Jesus. He isn't just in the Scriptures, He *is* the *Word*. Reading and studying His Word opens you up to receive Him. Through His divine Spirit into your thirsty soul, He pours, revealing His truth and His mystery a little at a time until you are entirely filled up. For as long as you continue to seek, He will never stop giving of Himself.

His generous gift of Himself to you accomplishes many things (some you can see but many you can't). He is making Himself visible in you and through you. The more you invest, the more He invests. The more you seek, the more He gives. And over time, both in subtle and in profound ways, you begin to look more like Him and less like yourself. You are made into an ambassador and an agent, a messenger, a teacher, a healer, a counselor, and a witness. You are whatever He makes of you if you earnestly seek Him, love Him, and relate with Him.

He Is in Church and Community

Yes, the flawed and imperfect church. Just as there is no one human being who is without flaw or without sin, there is no perfect church. Not yet. But the New Testament provides evidence that the church is a gem. The church is where Jesus can shine through groups of people gathered together in His name. Your church doesn't have to have a large congregation or a fancy steeple; in fact, it doesn't have to be in a building at all. There are small churches all over Africa that meet outside under trees with as little as five people in attendance.

Church is a place to learn, worship, and fellowship, but we should not limit our relationship with Christ to church alone. My pastor, Pete Wilson of Cross Point Community Church in Nashville, Tennessee, reminds us regularly that "real church doesn't line up in rows, but circles up in homes." Meeting corporately is precious and purposeful, but real community is between small groups of people who meet regularly to grow in the Word together, offer encouragement and prayer support, and inspire faith into action.

My favorite thing about going to church is the biblically based, inspiring messages taught by our pastors. They have true gifts for relaying the messages of Scripture in ways that both increase my wisdom and strengthen my faith. Attending church has also led to incredible relationships and serving opportunities that have helped me grow as a servant.

For many years I have been involved in community groups, mostly of women who gather with a focus on Christ and on growing as students and servants. Having a group of peers to share life with—including friendship, prayer, and support—has provided me evidences of Jesus in action. When we come together in love to support each other through *anything*, Jesus uses us to expose His love. When community exists to love and serve Him, He will be there. You will see Him.

You, combined with all His other faithful followers, make up His beautiful church, the whole body of Christ. Together, spread out through space and time, we are being guided to accomplish His plan, His will, and His divine purpose. We, the body of Christ, are glorifying His perfect name.

You Will Find Him in Prayer

As a child, I had several "empty" experiences with prayer and eventually gave up believing altogether.

I attended church several times as a child but was not "raised" in a church. My dad was not a believer and still is not. My mom is a Christian, but she did not like to go to church without my dad, so we rarely went. After my parents divorced, my mom and I "church shopped" a bit, but we never settled into a permanent church home.

I have many memories of my mother sitting in one of her favorite chairs or at the comfy end of the sofa with her Bible open and a pen in hand, studying God's Word. I remember her teaching me Matthew 18:19, "Again, truly I tell you that if two of you on earth agree about anything they ask for, it will be done for them by my Father in heaven," and asking me to apply this verse as a prayer for my dad to come back. My dad did not return to us, which made it difficult for me to believe in prayer or to believe that there could be a "greater plan."

My mom's emotional wounds seemed to remain for a really long time without healing. I felt hopeless. It seemed that Jesus just didn't show up for us after we had prayed for Him to. Our prayers hadn't worked. We bounced around to several holy houses, assuming He would be in at least one of them. But when He didn't show up, we just stopped looking for Him. In other words, we wanted answered prayers right away. We wanted "yes" answers that seemed practical to us, and we needed some quick fixes. I was essentially requesting miracles from a resurrected superhero I didn't even have a relationship with. And this was just the first of many heart-breaking situations in which I felt that Jesus didn't show up for me. Who has the energy or the hope to believe in a Jesus who doesn't even bother to show up and continues to allow horrible things to happen?

I'm going to guess that this looks a shade different for each person, because no two lives are exactly alike. But I'm willing to bet that you've also experienced many letdowns of your own. Maybe at some point along your journey you felt that God ignored your cries and pleas. As for me, I viewed Jesus as a "fixer" with a magic wand who could make everything better for me if He wanted to. I wanted Jesus to do everything. I wanted Him to fix my life, and more than anything I wanted Him to eradicate the pain. On some level I thought it might work like a magic trick. He would snap His fingers like a magician, and I would be happy. He would undo all of life's tragedies. In hindsight, I can see that I also thought of Jesus as a doctor. A doctor makes a diagnosis and then provides a remedy. If it's basic, that remedy requires not much more than drinking a glass of water and swallowing some pills. The symptoms begin to fade, and in a matter of weeks we have all but forgotten we were sick.

Jesus isn't really in the business of doing something forgettable, and especially not if we're just going to keep it to ourselves. If I can be blunt, I don't believe He is going to spend His power on something unnoticeable and easily forgotten, but on something that will be remembered, valued, and shared ,and that will help us to better understand how much He truly loves us. He wants us to be transformed through prayer, not unmoved. So I believe He wants to see us stretch, because He is already reaching. Do you want God to perform magic tricks, or do you want to meet the best friend of your life, a loving Father who will take you on the journey of His well-lit path instead of you trying to fight your own way through the dark woods? Thankfully, by His abundant grace, when we stretch a little He reaches back to us and takes our hand in His.

As a result of reaching out to Him, what I have learned through my prayer life is that I can feel His presence. Sometimes His answer is yes, at times it is no, and often it is "not yet." Jesus didn't deliver my dad back to our family (a no), but He did heal my and my mom's wounds. Jesus did prepare a husband and more children for me after I had finally realized and confessed that He was more than enough. Though for the many years I was alone, His no was merely a "not yet." And the precious Father delivered me safely to Africa many times so that I could serve in orphanages (a yes). Remarkably, in His transformation of me, He has shaped my heart to pray His will instead of my own. When I am especially humbled and fervently seeking Him, His Spirit has directed my heart to lead my prayers. When you are truly open to receiving Him, His Spirit will guide your prayer life, and you will know it.

I love the beautiful picture in this verse of a child of God reaching out, stretching toward the heavenly Father: "Let us then approach the throne of grace with confidence so that we may receive mercy and find grace to help us in our time of need" (Hebrews 4:16). Did you see that? We approach the throne—whether we walk, run, crawl, jump, fall into or reach out, we can confidently move toward Christ and receive His grace and mercy. He may say no when we are self-serving, confused, unprepared, or out of line, but He will never say no to prayers for grace and mercy. When we bend, stretch, reach, and extend to Him and extend ourselves *for* Him, we can do so with such confidence that He will respond swiftly.

I used to misunderstand prayer to be a one-sided conversation, or more truthfully like a short, childish presentation. I could imagine myself like a little girl dressed up in delicate, frilly fabric, walking out on a stage before a darkened and empty auditorium with a bright spotlight, talking to the floating air particles. I would blurt something out, aiming to convince, and walk away hoping for the best. If I'm honest, I still feel childish and uncomfortable at times, but this picture does not remotely resemble right thinking about prayer.

First, prayer isn't something we have to get dressed up for, because He accepts us just as we are, right where we are. Second, the spotlight is on Jesus, not on you or me. He doesn't need us to be convincing but only to be willing to receive Him. And finally, when we seek communication with God through Christ, we are not speaking into a darkened, empty nothingness, because when we pray in Jesus's name, every word is heard.

Jesus teaches us how to pray in Luke 11:1-4:

One day Jesus was praying in a certain place. When he finished, one of his disciples said to him, "Lord, teach us to pray, just as John taught his disciples." He said to them, "When you pray say: 'Father, hallowed be your name, your kingdom come. Give us each day our daily bread. Forgive us our sins, for we also forgive everyone who sins against us. And lead us not into temptation.'"

His teaching reminds us to seek God's will first rather than to present our personal will to God and ask Him to approve it. When we ask God for our daily bread, we are essentially asking only for provision for that day, for God to deliver what we *need* (no more no less), which may not necessarily be what we *want*. In this, we seek to trust that He knows what is best for us. I am ever grateful for the careful reminder in these verses that forgiveness and temptation may be regular issues. Every day is new, and while I have already been forgiven of the sins I have confessed before

Him, I will always be a work in progress, so I need to remain alert to the temptations and influences that persuade the condition of my heart.

As I have now learned, prayer is not simply a time to make requests of God to do the things that we believe will make life easier or happier. God desires to be our peace and He is not likely to send us a substitute for that. He is *everything,* so if we cannot be satisfied in Him, it is not likely that we will *ever* be satisfied. Asking God to accomplish tangible things probably shouldn't be our primary focus. Asking God how you can accomplish tangible service for His kingdom, now that is a great start. When we pray "Your kingdom come" we are essentially acknowledging to God that we *know* He is in charge and that we *want* Him to lead because we trust that His will and His ways are far superior to our human schemes and understanding.

Back to my vision of a little, well-dressed girl pleading into a spotlight. I used to feel that God's will didn't require my participation. I may have entertained in my mind that He was a master strategist orchestrating every move and that I was a pawn, standing still. He *is* the master of all creation and He *is* the great orchestrator with sovereign and providential power, but if I am guilty of just praying and then waiting around for Him to make the next move, I might fail to recognize that He has prepared a role for me, a purpose in His will, and that He gives me opportunities to be an obedient and willing participant in His plans. When we pray for "God's will," we can understand that He may equip us to participate in His will as it is being carried out. We aren't pawns; we are precious persons empowered by His Spirit to walk in alignment with His will, which is to be carried out here on earth, just as it is in heaven. He has designed a part for each of us.

I have also been guilty of viewing God as a waiter, complete with pen and paper jotting down specifics. I'd place my order, wait for a while, and eventually it would all show up precisely per my detailed request. But He isn't a waiter. He is more like the developer and manager of a massive building project, and I've been given the opportunity to help unload bricks. Will the project be accomplished if I don't show up? It will, but when I show up, I become a part of the process and the subsequent progress. When I show up, I not only get to watch it all falling into place one brick at a time, I also get to help lighten someone else's load. Praying is one way we can "show up." Praying for His will to guide your life is like "showing up" and being willing to move one brick at a time with the anticipation that the finished product will be a glorious monument to the Lord of all.

Think of God as a face-to-face friend. When you meet with a friend, do you forgo the greetings and instantly begin asking for favors? Typically, time spent with friends involves sharing life situations. If it's a healthy, balanced friendship, you do some talking and some listening. You may encourage each other, compliment each other, and share hugs and "I love yous." Hopefully you affirm each other in good ways and you aren't afraid to approach one another when serious situations arise that need to be discussed and worked through.

God desires true relationship with you in your prayer life. He wants to hear from your heart. He doesn't want you to memorize prayers that mean nothing to you and that you repeat monotonously as a task or a chore. He desires that your words to Him be from your heart and sincere, even when adapting Bible verses into your prayers. Take time to notice God and tell Him what you see. Discuss your sin with Him, and ask Him to forgive you and to heal you from that sin. Tell Him what you want from Him and what you want *of* Him. You can't know what you want *of* Him if you don't know what He is capable of, so it is important to study the Word and incorporate it into your prayers.

Are you hurting? Tell Him. Ask Him to teach you something through the pain and deliver you to the other side of it in a way that glorifies Him. Are you grateful for something? Tell Him. Did you have a quiet and peaceful drive into work this morning? Thank Him for that. Did your dinner taste especially delicious? Thank Him. The beauty in the trees to the flavor in your coffee, the phone call from a dear friend, the Christmas bonus, the soft rain on a Saturday morning, the joy of a friend—all of these things are worthy of praising Him about, so praise Him. You could praise Him all day long.

My first prayers as a new Christian were all prayers of praise and gratitude. I didn't know how to talk to Him, but I knew how to thank Him. I knew to tell Him that I wanted to make Him happy and to be closer to Him. I knew I wanted to be more like Him and I wanted to be on my journey with Him. I knew I wanted Him to be in charge. I knew I wanted to behave well and I wanted to be forgiven and changed. I just told Him what I knew. Most of the time I spoke out loud to God with my eyes wide open, looking around for the traces of Him. I believe that the more I praise Him, the more He wants me to see of His mystery. It's a sweet exchange.

Scripture also teaches us that the Spirit intercedes for us, praying on our behalf: "In the same way, the Spirit helps us in our weakness. We do not know what we ought to pray for, but the Spirit himself intercedes for us with groans that words cannot express. And he who searches our hearts knows the mind of the Spirit, because the Spirit intercedes for the saints in accordance with God's will" (Romans 8:26-27).

It is important here to note that the "saints" defined in many Bible references means all who believe in Jesus, regardless of their character or spiritual maturity. Jesus, through His Spirit, carries our prayers to God the Father. He prays for us in our darkest moments when we haven't the strength to pray at all. But when we have the strength, He wants to know that we know what our sin is. He wants us to confess to Him and to seek deliverance, because in Him is the power to overcome.

Acknowledging sin, confessing it, and surrendering yourself might be a long process and that is where the stretching can get extremely uncomfortable. But it is necessary, and the result is freedom. If we fail to present our sins to Him, He doesn't necessarily have to listen to our prayers. The more raw and sincere you can be when you confess your sins, the more He desires to complete your transformation and give you real kingdom work. He just can't send an oblivious sinner in denial out into the world to represent Him. He can send only forgiven sinners out on His mission, and sinners can be forgiven only if they are dealing with their sin before God.

God will forgive you instantly, though your healing and transformation may be a slow process, one day at a time. Being freed from your sin might require intentional refrain; strength gained in the stretch. With God's power, this is possible. Talk with Him, and let Him move His power through you one day at a time to overcome, be transformed, be renewed, and be restored to the you He always intended you to be. The you that looks like Him. The you that is His reflection.

There will be days you don't stretch. There will be days you feel like hiding and you continue to struggle with sin. You will fail something or someone. You will be challenged or called into question. You may be ridiculed, and you may lose some friends. Make no mistake; stretching changes things. Being committed to continual physical stretching produces changes in physique. Your body becomes leaner, stronger, more defined, and more flexible. Physical stretching requires increased discipline, self-control, and focus to accomplish, but it is worth it. Stretching toward Jesus provides similar results in your faith, hope, and love, and in your overall spiritual transformation.

I'll be honest. Jesus is going to send you His Holy Spirit, and the Spirit is gonna trim some fat. Some of the unhealthy stuff in your life is going to have to be worked out, and it will not be easy. It can be joyful, and it can bring peace, but it will not be easy. Whatever you are addicted to—anything from narcotics to approval—will have to be surrendered every new day. Whatever you are worshipping—from money to your dreams—will have to be replaced with Jesus and His purpose. You will never be perfect. And you will never feel worthy of what He begins to do and continues to do in your life. You will always wonder why He chose you, and at times you will doubt.

But every trial you wade through waist deep and every moment you suffer for Him will produce in you an endurance to keep stretching toward

Him and *for* Him (on His behalf in the world). You will persevere. He will mature and ripen you, and according to His very Word, you will not lack anything. You *will not lack* anything. You will not lack *anything*. This is His power.

As James wrote, "Perseverance must finish its work so that you may be mature and complete, not lacking anything" (James 1:4). Stretch. He is so worth it!

CHAPTER 10

ROTATE

P ivot. Face Him. Rotate your position. Turn around. Look toward the
Son. This is the beginning of obedience. *Declare* your obedience so
this can be said about you: "You have declared this day that the Lord is
your God and that you will walk in obedience to him, that you will keep
his decrees, commands and laws, that you will listen to him" (Deuteronomy 27:17).

Before you accepted Christ, you couldn't have possibly been walking
in His ways. You were walking on your own path, deciding your direction
day by day. You made decisions with your own mind, or you followed
those who influence you the most, for better or for worse. You reacted to
your circumstances. You allowed yourself to be swayed by emotion or by
logic, for better or for worse. Either way, you were making decisions based
on earthly values, desires, or selfish ambition.

In my opinion, the most amazing gift that falls upon a new believer
or a prodigal returning to the Father is the immediate beginnings of the
transformation of the spirit. Paul wrote about what this transformation
looks like:

You, however, are controlled not by the sinful nature but by the Spirit, if the Spirit of God lives in you. And if anyone does not have the Spirit of Christ, he does not belong to Christ. But if Christ is in you, your body is dead because of sin, yet your spirit is alive because of righteousness. And if the Spirit of him who raised Jesus from the dead is living in you, he who raised Christ from the dead will also give life to your mortal bodies through his Spirit, who lives in you. (Romans 8:9-11)

At the age of twenty-nine, I was saved by grace through faith. Prior to then, I thought I had always been a believer, because I had been told about Jesus and had accepted the stories about the virgin birth, the crucifixion, and the resurrection. Hearing some accounts of the gospel and believing it was true made me also believe I was a Christian. Certainly the seeds had been planted, but I hadn't been transformed. In retrospect, I realize that I had only been a person who hadn't believed the stories were false; I had not even begun to grasp the power of the truth. If the Holy Spirit were contained in a syringe to be injected into my heart, that syringe was nearby, but I wouldn't receive it until my faith stretched beyond merely believing the stories weren't false.

The Holy Spirit makes us new. Something about our total internal composition will never be the same.

So there I was, facing a painful divorce and my umpteenth failure in multiple areas of my life. And I was brought to my knees by a power outside of myself. It was undeniable. As I picked myself up off the tear-drenched carpet inside my half-empty townhome, I knew I was different. I knew I was not myself. My faith was finally real. It had to be. I had given up on *me*.

My life began to change immediately. I did not gain popularity. I did not get rich all of a sudden. All my ailments were not instantly healed. Every broken relationship wasn't automatically restored. But what I did begin to experience was far more exciting: Jesus became the focus of my heart and mind for nearly every waking moment. I could not get Jesus off my brain. I still can't.

I went to work every weekday and had to park in a lot about four blocks away from my downtown office. Those four blocks would change my life, day by day, for the next year or so. Every morning, that walk was my prayer time. Every afternoon, that walk contained my moments of gratitude. I walked those walks with Jesus.

I also can clearly remember taking steps along the sidewalks and crossing busy streets, thinking about the Christians I knew and deeply admired, wondering if I would ever (e.v.e.r.) have a heart that resembled theirs. These people were the examples of Jesus in my life. They displayed love when it didn't make sense. They gave more than they kept. They smiled in the face of adversity. They rebounded instead of shattering into millions of little pieces. These were the people who showed me Jesus in the human form. Would I ever be like that? Would those characteristics ever be used to describe me? I didn't know, but I had hope. And that hope was the spark that Jesus would fan into a flame, mercifully.

In the beginning it seemed like a mountain too high for me to climb. It felt to me much like other objects of desperate want. Before I was married, I worried: "Will I *ever* meet the man of my dreams?" Before I was employed, I impatiently wondered, "Will I *ever* get the type of job that I want?" When I was a new piano student, I entertained the question "Will I *ever* be a master pianist? " The answers to those questions could have been "maybe soon," "it might take years," or "maybe never." I wanted my transformation with Him to happen quickly, and I wanted it to be visible.

One major theme in my Christian walk would hover over me: Obedience. Obedience. Obedience. I didn't really recognize the importance of this or understand it at first, but that is one of the beautiful ways of the Holy Spirit—the power to draw us and attract us to Christlikeness. The Spirit provided some influences to help me begin to think and act like a disciple. The Holy Spirit rotated me toward the Son, turning me around and pointing me in the right direction. Eventually, His Spirit changed my way of thinking.

We are to be obedient in facing the Son. We are to be obedient in moving in the right direction and in "putting on the mind of Christ" (see Philippians 2:5-8). Obedience is not forced. You have to choose it. The Holy Spirit provides promptings, nudges, and convictions. The Holy Spirit sometimes whispers and sometimes shouts. "And this is love: that we walk in *obedience* to his commands. As you have heard from the beginning, his command is that you walk in love" (2 John 1:6).

The beginning of my surrendered life of living in obedience involved church. A lot of church. A wholelottachurch. I walked through the doors of a church near my house that I knew had a large attendance. I thought the larger the church, the less I would stand out. I was utterly confused in the entry foyer and the hallways. I had no idea where I was, where I belonged, or how I would maneuver this strange place filled with strangers. All I knew is that I was hoping Jesus was there and that I wouldn't be made a fool of.

At first I was impressed and hopeful that these folks were my kindred spirits. My prayer was that I would fit in and not feel like the stranger I knew I was. The pastor delivered a message of hope, and I was fairly hooked. The people were casual, not perfect. The pastor was charismatic and funny, not stiff and critical. It was really just what I needed. Before long I was attending church on Sundays and Wednesday evenings, and on Thursday evenings for the singles group. If church was a pill, I was popping it three times a week.

The messages were printed in outline form on a simple paper brochure, and I collected them. I took copious notes. I opened my Bible to the Scripture references and slowly but steadily began to have one aha moment after another. I'm sure the Holy Spirit loves young new believers like I was. Willing, ready, eager, and easily influenced. As to the Spirit, I was in the front row, with one hand raised and the other taking notes. I wanted everything the Spirit was willing to give me. Mine was a God-given hunger.

We have to recognize that we all have a God given hunger. He created us to be hungry for Him and for all that He offers. He created us to hunger for knowledge, for hope and understanding, and to be hungry for His comfort and compassion. This is all part of our rotation. As the sun draws and pulls the hungry flower in the pot on the window sill toward itself, the Holy Spirit draws us to the light of the world. A turn is mandatory. It must happen.

After attending church for a while, I began literally starving for more Scriptures, more sermons and prayers; more of God. I was already attending every service, and yet my appetite for more wasn't satisfied, so I began registering for Bible studies with home groups and service projects with teams from church, out in the community. By experiencing other Christians up close and personal, I began to learn something you simply cannot learn any other way. I learned about living. About serving, doing, giving, loving, forgiving, and not giving up.

I began to see radical faith and monumental love. I would see one person break while another helped to put her back together in love, with Jesus being the glue. I would see one person fear while the other administered calm and hope. I began to see anger and bitterness transformed into selfless surrender. I saw each of these things in the name of Christ. Why? Because those people had already been snagged by the Spirit and were doing their best to live in obedience to Him. They had surrendered their lives to Christ and somehow understood that this life wasn't about them. Somehow they had discovered that they were agents of Christ's love, and they were doing their best somehow, naturally, to live life like He would. Unfolding in front of me was evidence that God prepares and equips His children to carry out His mission, to fulfill His purposes for His glory.

It seems simpler in words than it is. It is not as if this all came together for me in one bold strike of lightning to my brain after a brief series of special moments. Not of the rapid sort, these recognitions approached me as a slow epiphany. I wasn't eager to be patient for the transformation. I'm not even totally sure I believed in the transformation. Maybe I had believed a part of me would always feel broken and battered. Maybe I didn't even have hope for a total transformation. Any transformation takes time. It takes time to lose weight. It takes time to build muscle. It takes time to increase strength and endurance. You first have to commit to the work, then you have to follow the steps, and then you have to recognize the evidence.

By far, the two most powerful exercises in my spiritual life affecting my rotational transformation have been group Bible studies and personal prayer journaling. I have been committed to the Bible studies for many years now and cannot imagine life without them. Prayer journaling has been a newer exercise in recent years, but through it I have felt the power and presence of the Holy Spirit. Through discipline I can surrender my will and seek God's alone.

Blessed are all who fear the Lord, who walk in obedience to him."
Psalm 128:1

Fruitful

It is in the rotation that you will begin to bear fruit. The word *fruit* conjures up a delectable flavor of natural sweetness.

Today, fruit is a part of my daily diet. It began years ago when my second and third children were born, as I was intentional about feeding them tons of sweet fruit in the hopes they would prefer it to unhealthy or artificial substitutes. I wanted them to crave and choose the good stuff.

There is just something incredibly glorious about biting into a perfect juicy pineapple or a sweet-and-sour black plum. Have you ever eaten a strawberry with such a precious flavor that all your troubles just disappear? There is nothing sweeter. There is no artificial sweetener or refined sugar product that can come close. It is no wonder that Jesus uses the example of the sweetest natural thing on the planet to teach us what he wants for us to produce: go and bear fruit. Paul wrote, "And we pray this in order that you may live a life worthy of the Lord and may please him in every way: bearing fruit in every good work, growing in the knowledge of God" (Colossians 1:10). God wants to see sweet juices dripping from our extremities, dropping onto the heads of the chosen that are still lost. His kingdom is gonna be sticky sweet, y'all. I just know it!

Rotate, Turn the Soil, Sow Seeds

For fruit to grow on a plant, the plant needs to receive sunlight. The earth rotates around the sun, and as a result, the plant receives the sunlight from all sides, from every angle.

Unlike fruit that must remain physically attached to a tree or a vine, we are mobile and detached. We may choose what we connect ourselves to or whether to be connected to anything or anyone at all. Our busy, technology-driven lives offer many distractions that can captivate our attention. If we are not intentional about connecting with Christ, we may find that we are like a branch that doesn't bear fruit, like a broken branch lying on the ground. Our branches are to remain connected to His vine. Only by remaining in Him, connected to the vine, can we ever dream of bearing fruit. Jesus said, "I am the true vine, and my Father is the gardener. He cuts off every branch in me that bears no fruit, while every branch that does bear fruit he prunes so that it will be even more fruitful" (John 15:1-2).

The plant in the window must be rotated for upright growth. Likewise, for us to achieve upright growth we must turn toward Christ and face Him. We must be intentional about remaining attached to Him.

Psalm 126 speaks of sowing: "Those who sow in tears will reap with songs of joy. He who goes out weeping, carrying seed to sow, will return with songs of joy, carrying sheaves with him" (vv. 5-6). Sowing in tears is a "got to" in Christianity. Sowing seeds bears a fruitful harvest. From a strictly human standpoint, we tend to sow first for survival and second for pleasure. We rarely think outside of ourselves or our immediate family, because what benefits one usually benefits the other. This is how we do life.

Turning toward Jesus means living life *for* Him. Who is Jesus's family? Potentially everyone, regardless of outward appearances, behaviors, or characteristics. Only God can know the heart of a person truly, so when we turn toward Him to live for Him, we have to treat everyone like a potentially saved, redeemed, restored, and transformed being destined for the heavenly realms. We are not permitted to write someone off, and we cannot declare anyone hopeless, because we simply cannot make any determinations about their hearts. Aren't you glad Jesus didn't do that to you? *Shew, I am.*

We have to be "about" the harvest of the kingdom of God. *Sow for a heavenly harvest.* I am convinced in my spirit that for each and every devoted believer and follower of Christ today, there was someone (or many someones) who planted seeds in each of them along the way. In the same way I believe that there was someone who sowed in tears for each one of us. Tears. For you. That requires depth of heart and soul. Is your heart and soul crying in its depths for the lost? For anyone? Stretch beyond yourself toward the mighty King of kings and sow in tears for withered souls, and reap a bountiful harvest for the kingdom. This isn't just part of the mission of Jesus. This *is* the mission of Jesus. This *is* the will of God.

"Rotating" is assigning yourself a new position. We spend much of life trying to move up, advance, surpass, reach new heights, and be elevated. What if your goal in this life was to put everyone else first and to make yourself least and last? What if you stopped living to please people and instead lived only to please God? What if you shredded your agenda, cancelled your plans, and announced, "God, I'm coming with you. Send me out on your behalf and possess me with your Spirit. I'm doing this life for *you!*"? Maybe it is time to step down and to make this life about

God instead of about us. When you begin to see this option as freeing rather than miserable, your rotation is spinning out of glorious control. Congratulations!

Ultimately God's will is not for my life but for His glory. The plan God has for my life is a by-product of the work He has prepared for me to do for His kingdom. When I focus my attitude, my heart, my desires, and my goals toward achieving the plan for His kingdom, the result will be peace, hope, and joy in *my* life. Jesus says, "Blessed are those who hunger and thirst for righteousness, for they will be filled" (Matthew 5:6).

This "rotation" isn't a checklist of "good works" to accomplish, nor is it a to-do list. It is a posture of faith and obedience. When we have faith in God, His truth, His Spirit, and His reconciliation and redemption through Christ Jesus, our automatic and natural response is to act these things out by modeling the love of Christ. Jesus was a leader, but He modeled love by being a servant.

Turn us around, O Lord, to face you and to move toward you no matter how far we may have to extend outside of our comfort zones. Replace our earthly agenda with the hope for Your kingdom and raise us in obedience to be servant leaders

JOURNAL ENTRY

~ BIG PICTURE, LITTLE PICTURE ~

I woke up early this morning and took a shower while the rest of my house remained dark and silent. Joe had already left for work, and all three of my sons were upstairs tucked away in their comfy beds, resting snug. The two little ones have sweet pajama sets, and they went to bed with clean booties and clean feet. They went to sleep with clean hair and full bellies. They were tucked in with loving arms and prayed over. My oldest showed up after dark and did whatever he did while the rest of us slept. But he, too, fell asleep in a loving home, where he is always welcome. When I wake up each day, they are my big picture. In a sense, they are my whole world.

As I approach my second trip to Zimbabwe, where I will reconnect with most of the children I connected with last year, my picture starts to shift. I stand in the shower and massage my scalp with suds from a beautiful-smelling shampoo. I cleanse my face and pray that it might start looking younger. I maneuver around the tufts of fat around my gut as I lean and reach to shave stubbly hair from my legs. With every stroke and movement of what amounts more to vanity than it does to hygiene, I see that I am one body, in one house, in one subdivision, in one community, in one city, in one state, in one country on one continent. I am one teeny tiny fragment of a spirit in this world. This world is so big. And for whatever reason, I think *my* family is the big picture.

It so isn't.

Soon my heart and mind will race with anxiety and anticipation as I prepare to return to Zimbabwe. Why? Because I am forced in both exciting and uncomfortable ways to accept (again) that this life I am living isn't about me. It isn't even about my children and my other very treasured relationships. It is mostly about being willing to go where God is leading me, trusting that He has a reason and that I may never even fully know what that reason is.

It is about His big picture.

His big picture includes every people and every nation. His big picture is to complete every work that He has started to achieve precisely the purpose He intends. I believe that it is for people to know who He is, that He loves them, and that we're really all orphans up for adoption. He's busy doing all the heavenly paper-work to become our Father forever. I can share this on my blog. I can share it on Facebook. I can share it with my neighbors and weird drugged-out girls in the grocery store (true story). But for some reason (I don't need to know), He is making it possible for me to go to the ends of the earth where food and water are scarce, HIV is abundant, hope is fading, and love is thin. And I get to beam with light and joy for all that He is willing to do for them. Not me, them. I get to share His light in some of the darkest parts of the world. And for the moments that He does, I am just pretty overwhelmed that He allows me to have some glimpses of His big picture. And oh how different it looks. I cannot believe He does this for me. I am so flawed, so unworthy, and so small and faint, but He sends me anyway. I cannot fathom that He trusts me to spread it around His Word and His love. *Wow*, people, *wow. . .holy wow!*

So, my kids are my big picture because, in a sense, they are my whole world. *His* kids are *His* big picture because the *whole world* is *His*. We're all invited. Period. My prayer is that we could all look through His lens with His intensity to see His big picture. We might start doing life differently, every day. Not that our lenses aren't important, just that they are only snapshots.

Zoom out.

See more.

It's really big out there, and God cares about every square centimeter.

Oh, Jesus, I want to curl up in Your lap and look at all of Your photo albums with you. I want to see Your Shutterfly photo projects. I want to see what You care about, through Your lens, in full focus. I want to hear the stories of all the ways You love our children, whom You've fully adopted into Your heart and spirit. I want to see the scenes that make You weep and the moments that utterly crack You up. And I want to be in Your photo album too. I love You, Lord. Thank You for the big picture. Amen

About Face

We are an army of ambassadors. I can't help being giddy about how this works. I'm so crazy about the God of the universe and how this all plays out. He is brilliant. Magnificent. If I didn't know who I was then compared to who I am now, I'm not sure I'd believe in God. Oh, I know this world is full of faithless people. And I get it. I don't like it, but I get it. But by some supernatural miraculous mystery, I fell to my knees, sobbed on my carpet, and rose up a new creation. In an instant I did an about-face. Only I didn't move myself; He picked me up and turned me right around.

And I've been facing Him ever since. I'm in His army. And in a way, it is war. A war against evil. A war against sin. A war against hopelessness. An entire army of believers represent Christ in this world. He has individually gifted us and carved out our spaces. He sent His Spirit to dwell within us, and each time we seek Him, His very Spirit moves us through transformation. We are taking Him to the world. Oh you can be sure He is going with us, but we are marching with our feet. *Our beautiful feet.* That's what we read in Romans: "How, then, can they call on the one they have not believed in? And how can they believe in the one of whom they have not heard? And how can they hear without someone preaching to them? And how can they preach unless they are sent? As it is written, 'How beautiful are the feet of those who bring good news!'" (10:14-15). And in Isaiah: "How beautiful on the mountains are the feet of those who bring good news, who proclaim peace, who bring good tidings, who proclaim salvation, who say to Zion, 'Your God reigns!'" (52:7).

Paul said we are His ambassadors: "We are therefore Christ's ambassadors, as though God were making His appeal through us" (2 Corinthians 5:20). You betcha! You and I and all believers worldwide are the voices of His words. We've got to rally the troops because the enemy (Satan) is marching too. We must lean, stretch, rotate, and grow!

A Note about Satan Marching Too

According to the Word of God, the devil "masquerades as an angel of light" (2 Corinthians 11:14). Satan's aim is to choke out our hope. He is tossing poison into the garden, planting weeds, and infesting our petals with disease. The devil has many clever ideas, and if we are not shrewd, we will fall for his trickery. Satan's term will eventually come to an end, but until then we must be aware that his presence continues to do damage. Chapter twenty of the book of Revelation describes Satan's doom.

CHAPTER 11

GROW

My prayer is that by now we are able to see that there is direction for us, given in His Word, and also that there is a pattern to the path we follow. We have established that faith is the result of genuine belief (not merely words or a statement), a true opening of the heart and mind to be transformed. Romans 12:2 says, "Do not conform any longer to the pattern of this world, but be transformed by the renewing of your mind. Then you will be able to test and approve what God's will is—his good, pleasing and perfect will."

We have seen that the Lord designed each one of us intentionally and with purpose. We are beautiful even though flawed and imperfect. He is working on us and through us to expose the love that He is and to shine His light through us to illume His glory. He is making us magnificent in His sight and tending to the weeds of evil that threaten us. He is doing so by the power of His Spirit, and He is receiving our prayers through His precious son, who is 100 percent for us. Like a potted plant perched on a window sill, we can simply lean in to receive His nourishment. We can press into Him with all of our faith, because He can handle the weight of all that we carry. We need only to give it to Him.

We have explored the stretch—how we are transformed in reaching and bending toward Him. We can now recognize that life lived in His will is often outside our comfort zones. Reaching and stretching toward Him naturally change our perspective. We understand that we may have spent a significant chunk of our lives not facing Him at all, but rather going our own way and seeking our own reflection. To live for Christ requires an about-face; a pivot or rotation, and movement in a new direction. Moving toward God and His kingdom amounts to setting our own agenda aside and beginning to see this life through His lens instead of our own—and zooming out instead of in. It means putting self aside and striving to serve God instead of man.

Each of these elements—the lean, the stretch, and the pivot—when put together into an exercise will result in growth. We will grow in wisdom, in faith, in love, in compassion, and in Christlikeness. We will not stop growing until our heavenly Father decides it is time for our blossom to join His kingdom's bouquet.

And Speaking of Bouquets. . .

I am an amateur gardener. In fact, I haven't a clue what I am doing out there in the dirt, but I do love it so. I've made an honest attempt to cultivate beautiful roses (ack, haven't we all?), and they are mostly dead at this point. I have made a lot of mistakes (ack, haven't we all?). At first I planted them too close together, crowding them and making growth awkward and funky at best. I failed to tenderly treat their leaves against disease. And my awareness of the thorns never stopped me from touching in the wrong places and bleeding profusely more than once. Roses didn't work for me. And I didn't work for them.

So, now my flower garden is a hodge-podge of random plantings that do not make sense. It's wild, vibrant, exciting, surprising, and a lot of work. An expert flower gardener would most likely not be impressed with my efforts. But other gardeners' opinions really do not have to matter to me. I am "the gardener" of my garden. It is mine, and it only has to make sense and be beautiful to me. Now, I don't have a master plan like the Creator of the earth did, but I did create my garden for my pleasure and my enjoyment. In this situation, I am the only one who matters. My opinion counts above all because my garden is for me. It is mine.

We, His gathered bouquet, belong to Him, and He counts us as beautiful. We are the seeds that God has planted, and our growth matters very much to Him. He wants us to blossom and bear fruit. His strength is present to eliminate the weeds and prune the lifeless. Growth is so critical to this journey. He will cut back what is not fruitful in us. Whether we notice it or not, He removes the weeds that threaten to choke us. At other times He may allow us to wither a little and then bring us back to life just as we display a single droplet of faith. It doesn't all have to make sense to us, but we can grow in peace knowing that it does make sense to Him. Each one of us is unique in beauty and purpose, and we form together—the whole collection of us—to display the glory of His beauty as an unimaginably stunning bouquet.

In my quiet time this morning, as I reflected on personal growth, God undeniably presented an image in my mind's eye of myself. He showed me a cradle of grace; I was cupped in His mighty hands like a tiny baby. All my sins had been washed away, and I was innocent in His eyes. He is raising me up mercifully with abounding love and has attached me to His body along with the whole of His faithful servants. I ache for the detached; the ones who do not yet know Him. The baby cradled in the cup of His mighty hands is not the symbol of a newborn, but a symbol of the newly *reborn*. We all start off like babies, but breath and air and spirit and faith enable us to grow and mature. He disciplines us, guides us, and matures us in time. He nourishes our hearts and souls and forever pours in His true and Holy Spirit. This is how we grow.

But why do we have to grow? Why can't we just stay cradled away in His warm palm? Why can't we just praise Him and worship Him in solitude? Why can't we just go to heaven right now? Because my growth and your growth offer a benefit and purpose to His kingdom. He has prepared kingdom work for each of us to accomplish (see Ephesians 2:10). I'm not as much of a benefit to the kingdom in church on Sunday as I'd like to think I am. I've been called to put my faith into action. As James wrote, "As the body without spirit is dead, so faith without deeds is dead" (James 2:26). May we grow to a level of faith that produces good works—together a fruitful vineyard.

You will know that you have grown in your faith and moved past the cradle when you wake up in the morning and recognize that there is work to be done for Christ. You realize and are affected by the fact that there are people who have never heard the gospel, or people who have heard it but rejected it. These people need to have more seeds sown in them, and you will know that you have accomplished true spiritual growth when you desire for them to be able to see His hands and feet in action through others. You will know that you have achieved real growth in your faith when you are eager to put aside materialism and the luxuries in this life because you are convinced that the greatest experience you'll ever know is already booked, in heaven, and you simply cannot top that here on earth and in this lifetime with any "thing."

You will know that you have grown when you rest in the assurance that you are whole even when you are broken. And when you have ceased kicking yourself for your past because you have received and believed in God's real and permanent forgiveness. And when you are able to grasp the joy and blessing of prayer and fasting, of realizing peace, believing in His purpose, knowing hope, and receiving joy. If you are leaning, stretching, bending, and pivoting toward Him, you are growing to maturity. If you know that no one is beyond redemption and that loving the Lord and serving Him with all your heart is really all that matters, your growth and maturity is evident. Congratulations, this is right where He wants you— and all of us.

"Is not this the kind of fasting I have chosen: to loose the chains of injustice and untie the cords of the yoke, to set the oppressed free and break every yoke? Is it not to share your food with the hungry and to provide the poor wanderer with shelter—when you see the naked, to clothe him, and not to turn away from your own flesh and blood? Then your light will break forth like the dawn, and your healing will quickly appear; then your righteousness will go before you, and the glory of the Lord will be your rear guard. Then you will call, and the Lord will answer; you will cry for help, and he will say; Here am I. If you do away with the yoke of oppression, with the pointing finger and the malicious talk and if you spend yourselves in behalf of the hungry and satisfy the needs of the oppressed, then your light will rise in the darkness, and your night will become like the noonday. The Lord will guide you always; he will satisfy your needs in a sun-scorched land and will strengthen your frame. *You will be like a well-watered garden, like a spring whose waters never fail."* (Isaiah 58:6-11, emphasis added)

I love the way God creates an image here of fasting as "doing" rather than "abstaining." Instead of fasting by giving up food, we are to fast by giving up ourselves. Instead of only worshipping in a building with a cross on it and singing songs (while noble, beautiful, and spiritual), this picture of growth into mature faith painted by our masterful Creator is one of worshipping Him by caring for others the way that He has cared for us. It is a picture of lifting the heavy, burdensome yoke off the oppressed. Whose load can you make lighter? Who do you know that could use a little freedom? Who is buried under the weight of a dark and heavy world? Who could use some light? Love God. Love others. Serve God. Serve others.

The plant grows. It increases in height and width, strength and beauty. It weathers drought and floods, dangerous winds and hard-hitting hail. For all that it survives and endures, and through every storm that it perseveres by its strong and determined attachment to its root, it rises to become a thing of breathtaking beauty. And when the sun rises on it in the calmness of morning, eyes that are open can see its splendor in its full maturity.

The sun rises every day. It brings light even when hidden behind clouds. Its light shines with persistence. God's mercies are new every morning without fail.

"I form the light and create darkness, I bring prosperity and create disaster; I, the Lord, do all these things. You heavens above, rain down righteousness; let the clouds shower it down. Let the earth open wide, let salvation spring up, let righteousness grow with it; I, the Lord, have created it." (Isaiah 45:7-8)

Growing Pains

There is not a formula or a track to growth that is free of pain. I can recall God meeting me in the midst of my mistakes over and over again and telling me through my conscience, "Melissa, it hurts because you are trying to control. I have to let it hurt you so you will want to stop and let Me guide you." Sanctification is God's way of growing us up. Sanctification is God transforming you and me to become more and more like Christ. And it is God's will that we be sanctified (see I Thessalonians 4:3). In other words, it is His will that you and I grow, mature, and be transformed to think and act like Christ for the purpose of fulfilling the destiny of the heavenly kingdom. We would be naive to think that this would be easy and painless. And He isn't just going to sanctify us a little, but a lot. Paul wrote to the church in Thessalonica, "May God himself, the God of peace, sanctify you through and through. May your whole spirit, soul, and body be kept blameless at the coming of our Lord Jesus Christ. The one who calls you is faithful and he will do it" (I Thessalonians 5:23-24).

The removal of our fruitless branches and our weeds, well, it's gonna hurt. And that is okay. I am approached at times by beautiful souls inquiring how I got through this or that hard time with a positive attitude and a smile on my face. I often ponder the same about others. How can her eyes smile with genuine love just days after she has buried her baby? How does she speak words of encouragement in the midst of my struggle when her own struggle is so monumental? Leaning, stretching, and pivoting toward God produces this. When we humble ourselves before the Lord and seek Him, He refines the areas in our lives that do not honor Him. Just as we might physically cut non-fruit producing branches from a tree, He sometimes forces pruning upon us in His loving Father-knows-best kind of way. This pruning may involve changes in our relationships and "weeding out" bad habits or downright bad behaviors. We are being trimmed back and pruned for our own good and for His glory.

When trees are pruned, they are suddenly able to sprout and blossom. The natural consequence of removing the bad is an unstoppable production of good. Growth just happens. We can moan our way through the pruning, but if we willingly participate in the leaning, stretching, and pivoting, we will humbly and graciously receive the growing power of the cut. It is a necessary part of the experience. At some point we will be able to look back and see very clearly how necessary the removal of something from our life was to make room for more transformation, more beauty. I urge us all to be grateful for this.

On the old piece of furniture that someone dismisses as junk, under the layers of varnish and gunk, are the natural wood grains and true, rich colors. The gunk has to be sanded and scraped off for the treasure to be revealed. God isn't only polishing us up on the outside and painting us pretty. He is also unearthing the beauty at the core of our being and finding us the way we were designed from the beginning. He is peeling away the outer worn out damages to reveal His own image that dwells within. He is bringing out more of Himself. Is it no wonder that Jesus was a carpenter?

The following two verses of Scripture bring me such comfort when I am going through a season of being whittled, stripped, pruned, and unearthed. I encourage you to post these somewhere for yourself and to inscribe them on your hearts so you will be equipped to bless others when they are being pruned. There is always a purpose to these things, and every bit of the experience is worth the process.

> I consider that our present sufferings are not worth comparing to the glory that will be revealed in us. (Romans 8:18)

Remember, the end of your story is glory! You are getting there. I am getting there. And there someday we all shall be, together.

> Endure hardship as discipline; God is treating you as sons. For what son is not disciplined by his father? (Hebrews 12:7)

If you are a parent or if you had loving parents who disciplined you well, you *know* this. I do not discipline my children to see them hurt. I discipline them so they will learn and mature. I want to see them make better choices and to know the difference between right and wrong. I discipline them because I adore every precious little hair on their heads, and I know that effective discipline is a layer of protection between them and the evil that lurks in the world. If I love my children enough to get their attention when they are at fault, I have to know that the oceans covering the earth could not begin to contain the love our Father has just for me and just for you. And just your neighbor. And just your coworker. And just your fiercest enemy. May we know this love and beg for it.

> *Heavenly Father, please discipline me until I can do nothing but stand upright in Your sight. Discipline me with hardship, heartbreak, and suffering. Strip away things I love, things I worship and idolize, even if it breaks me in two. Remove the earthly things that keep me from doing*

kingdom work. Remind me in Your love that this life isn't about this life. Jesus, Lord of lords, Prince of peace, Redeemer, Healer, and Wonderful Counselor, bring me to my knees in surrender, and rid me of gunk and grime. Make me grow small. Precious Jesus, I surrender in willingness to Your mighty authority, because you don't need my help driving this bus. One way. Heaven. No return. Amen.

JOURNAL ENTRY

~ THROUGH AND THROUGH ~

"May God himself, the God of peace, sanctify you through and through."
I Thessalonians 5:23a

Sometimes these words run through my mind: "through and through." They lead me to a myriad of thoughts. I picture a grocery store aisle. I'm searching all over for some random product. And what about that crazy spice section? Have you ever searched through and through to find something?

Sometimes I see the toy box. There is no counting the number of times I have searched through and through to help one of my kids find the tiniest toy on earth. At times I find cracker crumbs, remnants of broccoli, puzzle pieces—but oh for that tiny wheel or the shrunken little man that is supposed to be piloting the tiny little plane. Through and through I search.

Have you ever misplaced a treasured photo or a special letter? Have you searched the attic or the basement through and through, and gone through every box, so many times over and over, not willing to give up—to the point that you know by heart where everything is? Everything but that one thing?

Through and through seems so intense, so detailed; like nearly physically unearthing something. Doesn't through and through reveal so much? Maybe you find what you aren't even looking for. Or perhaps you clean out a bunch of clutter in the process.

What will He unearth if He searches me through and through? What will He find, or worse, what will He allow me to find that I had been trying to hide and deny? Maybe He will de-clutter me and remove the cobwebs. Perhaps He will begin to heal me and give me new life.

Sanctify means "to be made holy" or "to be set apart." And *sanctification* means "an act of God by which believers become more and more conformed to Christ's image."

I love the repetition of the word *through*. He will not just sanctify you and me. He will sanctify us *through and through*. He will search and shape every part of us. Everything broken. Everything small. Everything hidden. Everything dusty. Everything rotted. All things shredded. All things torn. All things missing.

There can be no such thing as external sanctification, only internal. And this process means that His Spirit is going to search us through and through. He will touch every aspect of our character, thoughts, heart, emotions, sins, and more. And as we are willing agents, this process will shape us more and more into the image of Christ Himself—not His external image, but His internal image. Our hopes will be more and more like His. Our love will be more and more like His. Our passion will be more and more like His.

We may be stretched and rearranged when He is doing His work, and surely by the time He is done. But in the "through and through," we will be "more and more." We will be set apart and holy.

Grow Small

As we watch children grow, we can see that they physically get bigger and taller over time. I'd like to suggest that growth in Christ over time helps make us *smaller*. The Bible doesn't instruct us to be first, biggest, and most noticeable. His faithful servants are taught to be humbled, to be least and last, small by comparison. Jesus said, "The greatest among you will be your servant. For whoever exalts himself will be humbled, and whoever humbles himself will be exalted," And "many who are first will be last, and the last first" (Matthew 23:11-12; Mark 10:31).

The huge, glorious, noticeable position is reserved for the throne of God. In I Corinthians, Paul teaches that we are servants of Christ and that we have tasks that are important, but God is in the spotlight. He wrote, "I planted the seed, Apollos watered it, but God made it grow. So neither he who plants nor he who waters is anything, but only God, who makes things grow" (I Corinthians 3:6-7). Paul went on to describe that the one who plants and the one who waters will be rewarded for their commitment to the cause, but they are not to take credit for what ultimately is the work performed by God.

Growing (or becoming spiritually mature) doesn't mean drawing attention away from God and onto ourselves. Our personal growth is not to be measured in "big and tall." In God's economy, maturity in Christ and growth in wisdom humbles us into smallness, into last place. I don't know about you, but this thrills me. Isn't much of our society in a competition to be noticed, admired, respected, adored, praised, and heard? It's a tough rat race out there, where the competition is fierce. Grace is our reward, and there is more than enough for all, because there is no competition in the kingdom of heaven and in God's economy. Our greatest acts of service are carried out in last place. Growth indicates humility. In fact, growth cannot exist without it and vice versa.

"But grow in the grace and the knowledge of our Lord and Savior Jesus Christ. To him
be glory both now and forever."
2 Peter 3:18

PART IV

~ Remember, Feast and Fast

Close the door to the past, but leave a window open.

Peering back onto your yesterdays allows you to see the redemption that led you to today. A significant portion of the book of Deuteronomy warns the Israelites not to forget where they had been with God and to remember what He delivered them from. God challenged them to remember—not to ever forget.

This message belongs to us also. Closing the door on our past doesn't honor the Redeemer, the One who rescued you. Closing the door silences your song. David sings many psalms in remembrance of God's protection and deliverance. To forget the depths of your despair is to deny that He raised you up and washed you clean.

Let us remember, O Lord.

Moses said, "This is what the Lord has commanded: Take an omer of manna and keep it for the generations to come, so they can see the bread I gave you to eat in the wilderness when I brought you out of Egypt." (Exodus 16:32).

CHAPTER 12

AWAKENING

One of my favorite secular songs is by Marc Broussard. As a musi-cian, Marc travels more than he is home. As is often necessary, he is busing away from his wife and child, a son named Gavin, for whom Marc penned "Gavin's Song" while on tour. It first caught my attention because of the amazing melody and vocal delivery when I heard him perform it live at Ryman Auditorium in Nashville, a venue filled with church pews. I was nearly brought to my knees in a crowd of thousands. This lyric did me in: "I wish you heartache that leaves you more of a man." But, instead of weeping and convulsing on the Ryman floor, attracting paramedics and such, I contained my inner devastation. When I got home, I purchased the download and cried for days and days and days.

See, this lyric rattles me for two very different reasons. First, it is sheer wisdom. Don't we know that heartache leaves us more of a man or woman? Well, sure, we can drown in the cracks and fractures that allow bitterness to well up and consume; or we can emerge pieced back together by God. So, I embrace every way that my heart has been shattered, because every time the Lord of all pieces me back together I am reinforced and stronger than ever.

The second way that this lyric rattles me is the bitter-sweetness in the truth of it and how that applies to my loved ones. In some ways, I want my children and all of my loved ones to experience brokenness because I want them to experience needing Jesus. I want them to participate in the leaning, the reaching, and the pivoting, and I want them to journey also to the well of living water. I believe that God will piece the brokenness of my loved ones back together into a masterpiece even more beautiful, very much because of the fractures they endure. Basically, if we have never been broken, we can never be healed. It is that simple. I want this for them and for me. I want the hand of God to piece me together. I want to be formed in the way that He has dreamed for me. How could this possibly happen if something within me does not shatter? And, people, I have been shattered!

Fractures

Please know that my life and my heart have endured multiple fractures and that I write from a perspective of having been mercifully saved and gently restored. I offer you a brief peek at some of the fractures that once left me shattered.

Two divorces. Fractures. The end.

Literally.

Like you, I do not appreciate when the things that I dream of lasting forever come to an end. I certainly do not enjoy experiencing the same trauma over and over and over again. But the Lord is present at the beginning of every ending. He does not abandon. He is hanging around with adhesive—His love that binds.

Betrayal by friends. Fractures. Whoa. Did not see those coming. Multiple times, Lord? Seriously? The first cut may be the deepest, but I could argue that multiple cuts require a graft. Grafting is the surgical process of transplanting living tissue for dead tissue. Repeated fractures can leave us dead on the inside if we do not turn to Him. He will graft Himself to us. He is the living thing that replaces the death in our brokenness.

Miscarriage. Another fracture. Oh, my soul—like an earthquake that opens wide the fault line, subjecting everything nearby to fall in and be utterly destroyed. Anything that shakes and rattles your world, causing it to come crumbling down, can leave you feeling incapacitated, unable to crawl out from under the rubble. The only way out is to be lifted. Lifted high. Cradled in holy hands. His palm.

Diagnosis. My third child was born with a condition not normally included in a prospective parent's ultimate dream. Who of us engages in reproduction begging the Father to bring us a human incapable of living up to the standards of society? Who pleads with the Father for a child with physical, emotional, and developmental disabilities? And how many mothers and fathers enter parenthood with the dream that the nest will never ever be empty?

Engulfed. Swallowed whole. Drowning in thick sludge. Frozen by fear. Head in hands or methodically thrashed against the walls. Utter despair. Death of hope. Fractured again. Am I ringing anybody's bell? You may have felt some form of this. Enter Down syndrome. Yes, my precious third child, Shawn, was born with Down syndrome. We had no warning. In fact, we didn't know at all until he was a full day old. For the first twenty-four hours of his life, he was everything we had ever prayed for. He was a healthy, normal little angel, because we didn't know that he indeed wasn't.

And then, out of nowhere, we were pulled under as if an unsuspected riptide were thrashing us around, disorienting us. We were unsure if we would ever breathe again. Drowning might have seemed like the safer option in those moments, but we caught our breath and were left standing to cope with ten gazillion unknowns. We were standing with paralysis and unable to take a single step in any direction.

Fractured? Uh, yeah, for a moment. Because as soon as the pain rushed in, He ushered it right out. Jesus, the precious Healer didn't undo Shawn's diagnosis, but He gently tended to our wounds until no sign of fracture could be found. He turned our worry into wonder and strength. He sculpted our grief into grandeur, and He affixed our shattered pieces into a new masterpiece. He caused us not only to rejoice in our son but also to rejoice in the wonders of His crazy love. God hadn't given us a lemon; rather He had gifted us with an opportunity that causes us to stand in awe and wonder at the mighty workings of His very intentional masterpieces—every baby.

Estrangement. To this very day I have loved ones that are not a part of my life.

Self-infliction. Some of the hardest fractures to overcome are those I brought on myself: pain from the ramifications of promiscuity.

Fractures, in the moment, are the extreme opposite of glamour. Scars are evidence of wounds. We do not like that our wounds are exposed. Society drives us toward perfection, especially with respect to outward appearances, and we have bought into this at a cellular level. We do not want anyone to see our battle scars. We do not want others to be able to count the fractures in our hearts. We are forced to believe that scars are ugly and that broken things should be disposed. Advertisers do not want us to fix what is broken. They want us to toss it out and buy something brand spanking new and to repeat the process often. Out with the old and in with the new.

Many of us do this with our material things, and often we do this with our relationships. Even if we do not toss out our friends and loved ones, we do continually search for ways to make them better, more perfect, new and improved. But the glory is this: we cannot be mended if we have never been broken, and we cannot be put back together in His image if we are not willing to be altered. To the Christian, an exposed fracture isn't ugly. It is evidence of a redemption story. Instead of trying to hide in shame, we need to be willing to uncover our fractures and allow them to be visible so that those who have not yet been mended can see the hope in how we have been raised up in one piece.

Jesus didn't avoid people in poverty. He mingled with them. Jesus wasn't afraid of lepers. He touched them. Jesus poured out His grace on a prostitute. Jesus's lineage came right through broken people. He was and is directly related to massive fractures. So, do you feel shame? Are you afraid of exposing your fractures? Are you worried about what the world will think? These things are a waste of your fears. Jesus isn't shocked by your brokenness. He just wants to restore you. And then He will want to use your story to get to the fracture of someone else. He is in the business of love and forgiveness, healing and restoration.

Can you receive His full forgiveness today and not look back in doubt about it tomorrow? Receive it, friends. It is free. He has paid a high price to piece you back together, and He intends to deliver you wholly into the eternal kingdom that awaits us. Leave your baggage behind. You are no longer shattered. You have been made spiritually new. Own it with a song on your lips. God is so good.

Journal Entry

Perpetual Time-Out

As children will do, my boys were making a lot of noise. They created sound effects for every toy and they persisted in their noise making. You didn't hear this from me, but boys and their toys and their sounds will annoy. You gotta love 'em and, boy, do I, but peace and quiet are rare luxuries. I have been known on occasion to receive such noise with frustration and desperation. I should invest in earplugs.

One particular day I negotiated for quiet and just couldn't strike a deal. After multiple attempts and at the end of my wits, my darling boys were sentenced to time-out. I knew that my tender Asher would eventually approach me with remorse and a deal, but until then, I would thrive in the silence.

Ten minutes into the sentencing, apologies began rolling off his tongue. He reached across my Bible and into my lap for the forgiving arms and the momma kisses. I set aside my Bible and embraced him even bigger than he expected. I always do. Forgiveness. A done deal.

Longer time-outs are more effective. More time to reflect. More time to burn and melt and cool and thaw. More time to process. More time to get it.

Fast-forward four hours. I am in the shower, washing my hair, minding my own business, and suddenly I began to cry a little. Abrupt and acute, it was a thirty-second cry, a quick and sudden release of whatever it was, followed by a fresh smile. I realized I am in time-out. God has lovingly asked me to sit aside in the quiet, unmoving, and think about my thoughts, actions, behaviors, words, and lack thereof. I have been in a God ordered time out.

With believers, He is a refiner and administer of discipline, not an angry punisher. He is a molder and a shaper, a potter. He wasn't harsh, and he did not scream. He placed me in a corner and is not going to let me out until I have fully reflected on why I am in time-out in the first place. Maybe I spent too much money on things I did not need. Maybe I haven't played the right role in my marriage. I could be working too hard on things that will produce too little. I could be ignoring His promptings, guidance, and leading. Maybe I am standing on my own instead of leaning on Him.

I am uncertain, and surely that is part of my trouble. This is not a matter of unrepentant sin but a matter of feet stuck in stagnant waters. I do ask of Him why this season of life is so hard. Why am I indecisive? Why can I not come up for air? Where am I supposed to be? What is missing? I talk to Him. I tell Him what I am learning. And then I beg, "Can I just get out of time-out now, God?"

He just keeps saying, "A little longer." But it is as if I am in perpetual time-out, thinking, reflecting, trying, searching, serving, loving, growing, and trying to discern where to go from here. Without options and in the silence, I am at a loss for where to go.

I learn so much in this season of life, facing the many things that multiply, drag, pull, and add heavy weight. I learn from the grief, the hope, and the despair. I learn from the love. I am learning to let my heart break for the things that trouble our God in heaven.

There are things I want to do and people I want to serve, words I want to write and praise I want to shout. This time-out is not a punishment. I am not in trouble. It is for my own good. Maybe if He lets me out too soon, my heart will explode and create a disaster. Maybe I am in time-out so my passion and emotion can be contained and released later in more manageable increments. Only He knows.

Am I thinking about what I am doing? Yes. Am I learning? Absolutely. Do I know where I'll go when my time-out comes to an end? No. But God does. And I know that before I go there, He will give me His embrace, even bigger and tighter than I ever expected.

JOURNAL ENTRY

I Am No Abraham

When God called out to Abraham to tell him that he needed to leave his home and go to a land that God would reveal to him, Abraham said "Here I am." Remarkably, Abraham obeyed. On tired feet, he walked. Abraham continued to obey God even during the testing of his faith and the instruction to sacrifice his son Isaac. Thankfully, His faith would determine that the sacrifice wouldn't be necessary. Even then, when God called out again to Abraham, the ready reply was "Here I Am."

Faith and obedience.

Faith and obedience.

Faith and obedience.

Faith, obedience, and a lot of nerve.

I am no Abraham. Yes, God led me to Africa to serve orphans, and I went and I keep going. But God did not call me to go to the airport and wait there for weeks, months, or years until He revealed which plane I was to board. And while the journey takes two full days of travel, it isn't the forty years it took for Abraham. And God has not called me to sacrifice my children on an altar, but merely to sacrifice some time apart from them to do His work in filling up the hearts of orphaned children. I am no Abraham.

The callings to journey with tired feet upon the mountains of tribes are my "here I am" moments. I'll be honest; there is nothing in my world more thrilling and rewarding than being obedient when Jesus calls. I wish it were a daily strength of mine. It is not. I do not always know where God is leading me. Sometimes I feel very confused and at a crossroads, not knowing which way to go. Other times I flat out dread going. Following Jesus is not a simple journey. It is not decorated with riches. It is not safe. It is not free from illness, void of devastation, trauma, loss, hurt, and tragedy. It is challenging, radical, and unknown. And it is the adventure of a lifetime.

I am no Abraham. I am not the father of many nations. I am Melissa, raised in a broken home, an only child, estranged from some. I spent years of my life making horrible decision after horrible decision. I have abused myself in many ways and have sinned wide and deep. But I gave my heart to Him, and He cleansed it and made me new. He rid me of the disease of myself and paved a new road. It is a bumpy road with steep climbs but I do know where it is ultimately going. I'm on the road to the land of milk and honey, and for me, that road winds through Africa. He gave me hands, feet, and a heart to love orphans.

Here I am. I am Melissa.

CHAPTER 13

FEAST

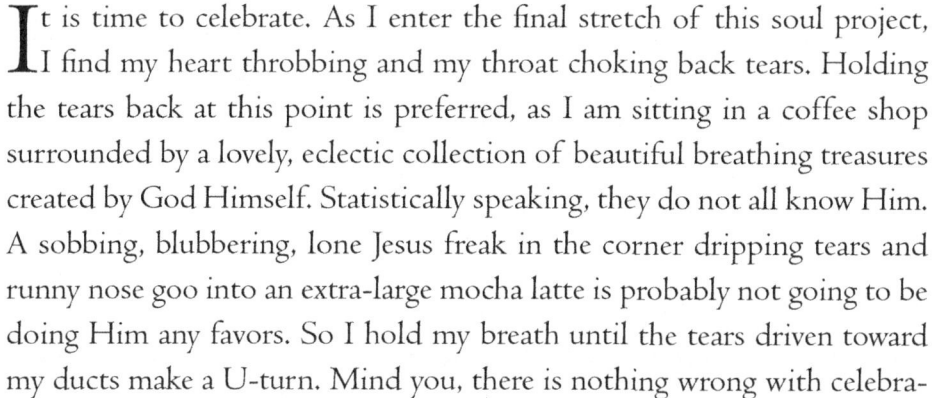

It is time to celebrate. As I enter the final stretch of this soul project, I find my heart throbbing and my throat choking back tears. Holding the tears back at this point is preferred, as I am sitting in a coffee shop surrounded by a lovely, eclectic collection of beautiful breathing treasures created by God Himself. Statistically speaking, they do not all know Him. A sobbing, blubbering, lone Jesus freak in the corner dripping tears and runny nose goo into an extra-large mocha latte is probably not going to be doing Him any favors. So I hold my breath until the tears driven toward my ducts make a U-turn. Mind you, there is nothing wrong with celebratory tears. I just want them to hold off for a bit. We have a little more to cover.

I love coming together. And I believe we are called to it. Throughout the Old Testament and New, many feasts are described. I may oversimplify this a bit and I beg in the Spirit that I will not demean or belittle a single act of spiritual, biblical feasting. Those feasts were intended for celebrating remembrances, making sacrificial offerings, and worshipping. There is nothing minor about any of that. The challenge is to consider whether or not we are truly participating in the act of "feasting", a celebration of our salvation and deliverance.

Consider this example from the book of Esther:

Mordecai recorded these events, and he sent letters to all the Jews throughout the provinces of King Xerxes, near and far, to have them celebrate annually the fourteenth and fifteenth days of the month of Adar as the time when the Jews got relief from their enemies, and as the month when their sorrow was turned into joy and their mourning into a day of celebration. He wrote them to observe the days as days of feasting and joy and giving presents of food to one another and gifts to the poor. So the Jews agreed to continue the celebration they had begun, doing what Mordecai had written to them. (Esther 9: 20-23)

This feast was a celebration of remembrance and of gratitude for all the Jews in their deliverance. God spared them from their enemies, turning their sorrows into joy and their mourning into a reason to celebrate. In turn, they celebrated. Together they enjoyed fellowship, food, and serving the poor by delivering gifts to those in need. In the same way, we are called to celebrate our salvation over and over again by coming together to remember. We must remember! We should break bread together. And not to be minimized is the act of rejoicing in such blessings by giving gifts to the poor. Those in poverty need assistance, and Jesus has sent us to tend to them in His name.

When you and I were destitute, all alone in our darkness, He showed up to feed us. He fed us hope. He fed us mercy. He fed us grace. In our deepest moan of starvation for salvation, He cupped our faces with one hand and drew a tiny opening of our mouths. He spoon fed us a dose of His living water. His water—the purest and holiest gift. He saved your life. He saved mine. We now hold this gift in all the filled-in holes of our heart.

And now that we walk in deepest gratitude, couldn't we celebrate by giving back? We must. We celebrate His love for us by giving to the financially poor and to the poor in spirit, for anyone without Him is poor indeed. I love that Mordecai instructed the Jews to give to the poor during their celebration. I find it most interesting that this idea was living in his heart and came out through his declaration. He didn't just make this suggestion because it sounded good. Mordecai was following God's promptings. God had placed that desire right into his heart. Mordecai felt a strong urge to celebrate by giving to the poor because God had spared the lives of his people. It made sense.

I had a similar experience very early on in my faith walk. I accepted Christ in my very late twenties and became a front-row, 100 percent, three-times-a-week attendee at church. Several serving opportunities came up here and there, and I was always drawn to anything that had to do with women in need and the homeless. The reason for the draw was simple for me to see. I didn't even need a rearview mirror. I had been a woman in desperate need, and although I have never been homeless, on more than one occasion I have come uncomfortably close.

I lived for a while in an apartment with no electricity. The power had been turned off, and my eviction notice was imminent. Rotten smells wafted from my empty refrigerator, and maggots were living in the thawed freezer, feeding on something that had spoiled. The only saving grace for us was food stamps and a mild weather pattern. My baby and I were able to eat nonperishables, and we had beds for rest. Otherwise we lived in darkness for about two weeks until an acquaintance with access to cash came to the rescue. It wasn't the same as sleeping in a car or not having a roof, but it was a version of hell to me, and I was living in fear. I remember those days well. They cause me to care.

I also remember my salvation, like it was yesterday. Twelve years later I am still celebrating on a regular basis. One of the very first precious things God did for me after I surrendered to His mercies and grace was to set my feet in motion toward serving the homeless. In other words, He caused me to celebrate my salvation by giving gifts to the poor. My oldest son and I began a three-year service relationship with a family shelter. It was incredible. God connected my heart and mind to their needs and longings. He met my celebration with their devastation. It was absolutely way far outside of the boundary of my comfort zone, but God does not call us to get comfy. He calls us to establish a feast of remembrance and celebration, a time to be so grateful for what He has done for us that we could think of nothing better to do than to serve others in the center of their despair.

With joy in salvation there is always reason to celebrate. There is always something of Christ to partake in. There will be no lack of reasons to gather together and praise His holy name in joy. Imagine you have just been notified that you won the lottery. Do you wait until after you've spent it all to celebrate? Or do you celebrate right away? I'm willing to bet you grab your nearest loved one, squeal at the top of your lungs, and embrace while simultaneously jumping up and down with shouts of disbelief, overcome with *joy*. Heaven is our jackpot, folks. Let us celebrate *now*. It is worth shouting about. And let us go ahead and spend some treasure on the poor in spirit.

Jesus said it this way:

"And do not set your heart on what you will eat or drink; do not worry about it. For the pagan world runs after all such things, and your Father knows that you need them. But seek his kingdom, and these things will be given to you as well. "Do not be afraid, little flock, for your Father has been pleased to give you the kingdom. Sell your possessions and give to the poor. Provide purses for yourselves that will not wear out, a treasure in heaven that will never fail, where no thief comes near and no moth destroys. For where your treasure is, there your heart will be also." (Luke 12:29-34)

We have inherited the kingdom, people. *We* have inherited the kingdom. We have *inherited* the kingdom. We have inherited the *kingdom*. For goodness sake, sing it with me . . . *We have inherited the kingdom!* If we can grasp the significance of this, we will not hesitate to sell our possessions and give to the poor. We will not frown to discover that earthly wealth and possessions are just not where it's at. Holla! Heaven is where it's at! Yep, Luke 12:34 is worth repeating over and over: "For where your treasure is, there your heart will be also."

Where is your treasure? Is it in the leather interior of your flashy European car? Is it dangling sparkly from your earlobes? Is it stored in your savings account? Is it invested in tech stocks—or whatever is promising to make you rich these days? Or is it stored in heaven? Where your treasure is, that is where your heart is. Your heart cannot be fulfilled anywhere on this earth, in this life. Not without Jesus. And if your heart is fulfilled in Christ, then your treasure can wait until heaven.

Back to feasting. Feasting is not to be confused with the act of over-indulging. That is not what we have been called to do. Remembering is a sacred act. Remembering keeps us coming back to our knees in prayers of gratitude; rejoicing anew in the celebration of salvation. This feast is about taking in pieces of Him and being joyful about it all. Feasting is an offering of love. May we never give up celebrating the love of our life. May the hallelujahs be too many to score. May the whispers of His name come together in a mighty roar.

The glory at the end of your story awaits you in a magnificent, majestic kingdom where hope never fades. Let your treasure be there, my friends. It is worth far more there than anything in the here and now.

༄

Fast

Fasting and mourning go hand in hand throughout much of Scripture, as do fasting and praying. Accounts of fasting are used repeatedly throughout all of God's Word to signify to us that it is a critical piece of this spiritual journey; this walk with Jesus.

Sometimes fasting is recognized as the observance that God can and will sustain us. That He is our nourishment and fullness. That He is our portion. We know from the book of Matthew that Jesus completed at least one forty-day fast. Fasting isn't indicated as one of the Ten Commandments, but since Jesus's lead is the one we follow, we should take note. The premise is that "going without" causes us to rely more on God.

Jesus paired His fasting with times of serious devoted prayer. Many Christians today practice fasting (privately) to seek clarity in hearing God's direction in certain circumstances. Fasting is a sacrifice. It speaks adoration, faith, and devotion to the Father. In his book *Celebration of Discipline*, Richard Foster wrote this about fasting: "Fasting reminds us that we are sustained by every word that proceeds from the mouth of God (Matt. 4:4). Food does not sustain us; God sustains us. Therefore, in experiences of fasting we are not so much abstaining from food as we are feasting on the Word of God. Fasting is feasting!"

I do not have a stellar fasting track record. I want to make it a regular commitment to practice relying on God for my nourishment by observing periods of fasting. He is living water, after all. I believe incredible opportunity exists specifically during periods of fasting. (Please research the proper way to fast before you try it.) Fasting as a discipline linked to the desire to draw nearer to God can result in heightened spiritual awareness. I believe it is where wisdom and discernment are doled out in heavy loads. Relying on God to be your provision and portion is an act of obedience that He is eager to bless.

> *[As a side note, I am sitting at my breakfast table as I write this section. A beautiful bowl of Honeycrisp apples is fifteen inches away in the two o'clock position. I was so mortified by the prospect of fasting again that I just reached in, grasped in desperation, and took four gigantic bites without so much as stopping for air. I nearly choked. The less I am able to fathom going without, the more significant a problem I may have. Somehow I embody the discipline to travel solo to Africa but lack the*

ability to wait till the end of a section on fasting to take a bite out of the very fruit that got Adam and Eve in boatloads of trouble. Suddenly I feel like I need a fig leaf. And another apple.

This is a disaster. An inner conversation is taking place in my mind, plotting to skip breakfast in the morning to see if I can just do a morning fast—a great starting point. I eat the same thing for breakfast every day. I spread some fresh-ground peanut butter onto a Wasa cracker and eat it with a cup of coffee. Actually, I eat two.

Right now, it is 4:23 p.m. on a Saturday, nowhere near breakfast. As my mind retaliates against the idea of a breakfast fast, my body begins to crave the PB and Wasa. It wants it now. Right now. I would like to know who opened up my front door and let the devil in—and just how long has he been here? And how did he sneak past the attack Pomapoodle?

Is this resonating with you? Am I the only one so addicted to feeding myself that I can't even trust God to sustain me? Rats!]

Here is what I know that I know that I know that I know: fasting is good. Jesus did it. We should too. Why would Jesus have fasted if it didn't stand to strengthen His relationship with God? Why would He have participated in it if it didn't serve a purpose to Himself or to His watchers or to the readers of His Word? Everything He did was intentional and had meaning. He instructed His disciples in fasting (see Matthew 6:16-18). Aren't we modern-day disciples?

Fasting isn't a practice that we should dismiss as being ancient or outdated. I bet many arguments could be made for fasting being more important in our present times than ever before. It may not have been commanded, but fasting is modeled to us through the Word because it must be significant and beneficial to our own faith experience. How much richer would our journeys to the well and the lowering of our buckets be if we were to approach the throne of grace on empty stomachs, filled instead with Him? How much less would we struggle to *see* if we were heightened to *hear*?

I pray that we can learn in obedience to sacrifice our stomachs in order to receive more of His heart. And while we are hungry, I pray that He would allow us to really *get* that there are millions of people on our planet starving every day. They lack food as a necessity while we overindulge in food as a luxury. I pray that we would hear Him say right to our hearts, "Remember, rejoice, and in celebration go give gifts to the poor."

∾

Sacrifice

[I am so thankful to have finally moved past that last section of writing. These cheese and crackers are so yummy.]

Beyond miracles, more awesome than walking on water and more astonishing than multiplying fishes and loaves, the most loving thing Jesus ever did was to sacrifice Himself for His children—you and me. He gave up His life. He endured unspeakable physical pain from heinous beatings while His blood poured out of throbbing lacerations. He took the place of our sins. Every sin of the world past, present, and future hung on Him as He hung on the cross. He bore the burden of sin in the world so that we could be free. He died so that we could have eternal life (see John 3:16).

Is it too much to ask that we carry some of the burden of the world now, for His children, for their freedom and in gratitude for ours, to the meager extent that a simple, forgiven human can? He has asked us to live our lives with servant hearts. He has asked us to grieve for what grieves Him. He has asked us to sacrifice so that the captive might be set free— free from hunger, starvation, loneliness, and poverty. I challenge us to see and accept that our wealth is literally killing people when we don't share. In our refusal to share, we have failed to sacrifice.

Jesus walked this earth in service of the kingdom of God without fancy threads. He had no material possessions to speak of. His ministry was to reach the lost and to share the good news. He modeled a servant's life for His disciples. Jesus inspired hope in everyone that He possibly could. Jesus *gave*. Jesus *had compassion*. Jesus blessed everyone who had faith, regardless of their sins. And while He was on this earth, He made a great case for feeding the hungry, serving the poor, and tending to the widows and orphans.

One of the greatest hypocrisy's of today's American Christian culture is that most of us solely serve ourselves. Only a very small percentage of us give even our pitiful leftovers to the poor. And only a fraction of those give sacrificially, not the leftovers but our first fruits. We make our house and car payments, send in the checks for our utilities (the blessed heat and water that we take for granted twenty-four hours a day). We pay for wireless Internet and game apps that involve ticked-off birds flying into little green pigs wearing construction hats. (I am guilty!) We pay a premium for coffee, purchase designer clothes for our children, and *then and only then*, if the starving kids in Africa *are lucky*, we send ten dollars and actually feel good about it.

But guess how many of them *aren't lucky?* That number is beyond our grasp of reality. According to statistics, practices, trends, and measurable data, we care much more about our comfort than theirs. We care much more about our nourishment than theirs. We care much more about our opportunities than theirs. In a nutshell, we just don't care much about them at all.

And we call ourselves *Christians*.

We claim to care about the things that Christ cares about. Go to church. *Check*. Read the Bible. *Check*. Pray often. *Check*. Huddle up in small groups. *Check*. Listen to worship music. *Check*. Sell your belongings and serve the poor. *Uh, what? Jesus, I'd really love to, but you see my children are wrapped up in T-ball and that gets really expensive, especially after you consider the cost of uniforms and snacks after the games.*

At what point are we going to own up to the reality that Jesus did not exclude us from His equation? When He instructed us to serve the poor, He meant all of us. When He commanded us to love one another, He didn't indicate borders. When He said, "Go out and be fishers of men" (Luke 5:10), He really meant to go. When He said that whatever we do unto the "least of these" we do unto Him (Matthew 25:40), He meant for us to love on them the way He would if He were still here in the flesh.

Now that He is in us, we are His flesh. We are His hands and feet. His sandals have been betrothed to each of us, and we have some walking to do. There are millions of us. We are equipped with His power and Spirit to handle His ministry. He handed it over to us. Are we participating? Or are we leaving it up to everyone else? Long ago I received a spiritual word of warning: *This isn't a group project where we all get the same grade.* We each have a role in this, so we should not abandon our call and just leave it up to the rest of the group.

But what is all of this "sacrifice" supposed to look like? I can tell you this much: tithing to any church of your choice is an incredible beginning, but to expect the church staff to take care of the rest is shirking responsibility. Supporting the church honors God. The church is His bride. He adores the church. He wants the church to survive scandals and false teachings. He has a vision for His church, and it includes heaven. Giving your tithe to the church enables the church to continue to preach, teach, and reach. Every church should have a giving plan that involves reaching out and serving out of love. The church should absolutely be serving humbly, coming to the rescue and delivering hope.

But let me make a case here for you as to why this isn't enough. If all you do is write the check to the church and leave the service and missions up to them, what is your role in the kingdom? Funding? Funding is good. Sacrificial funding is amazing and can be life changing. But Jesus was a mover. He didn't delegate spreading the message to others while He did nothing. He did it all. He was involved in intimate ways that far outreach dollars and cents.

This goes back to the biblical principle that faith inspires action. Sure, writing a check is an action—a significant action given the level of poverty in this world. But authentic faith should inspire us to care about where that money is going and what it is doing. Further, genuine faith will call us to get our feet wet and our fingers dirty. Humble faith will call us to dig in and not worry about the ache in our backs and the sweat on our brows. Somewhere in you is the Spirit prompting you to feed someone else before you feed yourself—and not to worry about it. Not even to give it a second thought. Just do it. That has been Jesus's motto long before Nike was on the world map. (No offense, Nike. I love your shoes. Also no offense to anyone whose health or physical condition keeps you from physically going out.)

> Jesus answered, "If you want to be perfect, go, sell your possessions and give to the poor, and you will have treasure in heaven. Then come, follow me." (Matthew 19:21)

> "He who gives to the poor will lack nothing, but he who closes his eyes to them receives many curses." (Proverbs 28:27)

Does tithing to the church cover it? I mean, with that *we're just good to go?* The call in Scripture to "the church" isn't necessarily a call to a congregation that lines up in pews. The church is not only a building with a steeple. The church is defined as the body of Christ. Belonging to or attending a church doesn't mean that we sneak in as noted servants under an umbrella of inclusion. If we aren't serving and giving, not coming to the rescue in the ways that we know we've been called, is it possible then that we aren't included?

God's character and Jesus's teachings about serving those in need is so prevalent in Scripture, we should consider what it may mean if we ignore them. Not feeding the hungry may be no different from walking up to a homeless, hungry person, showing him your wallet full of dollars, and walking away. Harsh? Yes,. because that is essentially what we do when we turn a blind eye, pretending not to notice. I can promise you they notice us. Not participating in the feeding, educating, or empowering of some the 150 million orphans in the world may have similar repercussions as looking one of them in the eyes and saying that you don't care. We may turn our backs and ignore the truth, but the truth isn't lost on *them*. Perhaps we also *shun* the opportunity because we are busy and we barely make enough to support our privileged lifestyles. Or we reject the idea that we are privileged because maybe we live paycheck to paycheck and this economy has been brutal. Our 401(k) is shrinking. At this rate, we might have to work until we are seventy. You know, at that *job* that pays a *salary*. Cold, hard cash. Where is the sacrifice in that?

Scripture teaches that we are saved by grace through faith, not by the good deeds that we do: "For it is by grace you have been saved, through faith—and this is not from yourselves, it is the gift of God—not by works; so that no one can boast" (Ephesians 2:8-9). We don't have to "work" for salvation, nor are we capable of "earning" it. Grace is a gift that we receive when we exercise faith.

So, with that as the focus, serving others has nothing whatsoever to do with the kingdom, right? Many like to argue that. But how does it make sense that we could extract this message of grace and ignore the rest of the teachings of Christ? Doesn't that just indicate that we either don't care about the rest or don't want to carry the burden? Scripture also teaches us that "faith without deeds is dead" (James 2:26). In other words, what good is your faith if you aren't doing good deeds? Faith should inspire good deeds. If there are no good deeds, there must not be authentic faith.

And the *numero uno* command in the New Testament is to love God and love others (see 1 Corinthians 13). Is it acceptable to ignore the "love others" command? It cannot possibly be. Because we are guided in wisdom to understand through Scripture that if we love God, we automatically want to love others. And if we don't know how, we seek the answer. We seek the direction and we look upon those opportunities joyfully. If opportunities are not knocking down our door, we go out in search of them. In the end, "each man should give what he has decided in his heart to give, not reluctantly or under compulsion, for God loves a cheerful giver" (2 Corinthians 9:7).

What if God had a plan for you all along? He does, "For we are created in Christ Jesus to do good works that God prepared in advance for us to do" (Ephesians 2:1). His plan for you was born before you were. Do you think love is a part of it? It is. And you can bet that His plan for you isn't packaged neatly in a simplified, safe boundary. His plan for you most likely stretches far beyond the zone of your comforts.

He provides for our salvation and prepares a home for us in an eternal heaven.

~ We celebrate.

~ We remember.

~ We feast on Him, on all that He provides, on His love.

~ We fast from ourselves, our agendas, from greed, anger, pride, and pretentiousness. We fast from anything that takes our focus off the glory of God.

~ We sacrifice and we walk. We love. We serve. We teach of His love and grace.

That is the kingdom agenda in a nutshell. Straightforward. Necessary.

Walk with Beautiful Feet

How beautiful on the mountains are the feet of those who bring good news, who proclaim peace, who bring good tidings, who proclaim salvation, who say to Zion, "Your God reigns."

Isaiah 52:7

"Everyone who calls on the name of the Lord will be saved." How, then, can they call on the one they have not believed in? And how can they believe in the one of whom they have not heard? And how can they hear without someone preaching to them? And how can they preach unless they are sent? As it is written, "How beautiful are the feet of those who bring good news!"

Romans 10:13-15

I was nineteen years old and very tender. Broken into a million pieces and raising my son by myself without many life skills. I had an immature level of belief in God and was not yet a surrendered follower in the Spirit. I was a whiner. But I knew about the starving children in Ethiopia. I had seen them on TV, and they broke my heart. From that moment on. I would hurt for them.

When I became a mother again at the age of thirty-four, the awareness was heightened in me to know that there were millions of children in the world without a mother. I would look into the eyes of my babies while my insides would wring and twist with a gnashing, excruciating throb over the idea that some baby somewhere had no mother to love her. I knew beyond a shadow of a doubt that God was calling me to serve orphans. And I knew He was calling me to start in Africa. Africa had been on my mind and in my heart for fourteen years. For me, the knowing was undeniable. He was sending me.

So I waited for an opportunity. And I waited. Waiting is easier than searching; it requires no energy and effort. And with waiting, if the thing you are waiting for never shows up, you can simply say, "It never showed up." But the Great Commission in Matthew 28:19 is to go, not wait: "Therefore go and make disciples of all nations, baptizing them in the name of the Father and of the Son and of the Holy Spirit."

I think I owe you an explanation of the wait. See, I have a church home that I love. It continues to be a wonderful church, fully immersed in serving God in so many ways, both locally and globally. But at the time of the most pressing call on my life, my beautiful church was not involved in any ministries in Africa, nor were they involved at that time in any orphan ministries. In the most simplistic explanation I can give you, I was waiting for my church to jump on board the African orphan train so I could hitch a ride. Much to my disappointment, it wasn't happening. My church was lovingly serving in the Dominican Republic, Haiti, and India. My African orphans were not on their map. But that didn't give me permission to give up.

So, I got a little crazy.

I came home from church after the new India initiative had been announced, feeling defeated and hopeless. I thought they had been about to announce a ministry in Africa, where mentally I had already signed up. Yes, Lord, make it easy for me! Instead, He whispered to me, "I never said it would be easy." I came home that day with my husband, my eighteen-month old, my three-year-old, and my eighteen-year-old and stated, "I'm going to Africa." Fortunately, God paired me with a husband who would not fearfully recognize the imminent dangers and who would also agree to support every hair-brained scheme I could concoct. That hubs of mine doesn't even seem to regret it now. Praise the Lord.

A World Wide Web search ensued, and soon I was depleted. I ran into so many dead ends in the search to fulfill my passion to go to Africa to serve orphan babies. I won't detail the list of disappointments, but just know that there were *many*. Eventually I located a travel agency that caters specifically to missionaries, pairing them with the specific type of mission they want to experience. And the great news for me was that they would help me as an "individual" rather than require me to be part of a team or large group. My criteria were simple: Africa. Orphans. I fielded these questions with these answers:

Planner: "What part of Africa?"

Me: "Any part."

Planner: "Do you wish to go on safari?"

Me: "No, I wish to serve orphans."

Planner: "Would you like to be near the coast so you can enjoy a holiday?"

Me: "Only if that is where the orphans are."

Planner: "All righty then."

Okay, she didn't really say that, but she got my drift. Soon I was contacted about a Christian ministry in Zimbabwe that serves orphans five days a week. Would I be interested? Yes, book the flight.

At this point, friends, I didn't even know where Zimbabwe was, and I was completely horrified after looking at the world map that hangs in my garage. My fear of flying had led me years earlier to vow that I would *never* fly anywhere that required more than three hours on an airplane, including boarding, taxiing, and deplaning. Besides being a weenie in general, I am also claustrophobic. Nothing about flying was glamorous or even *okay* with me. Yet I had just booked a flight all the way across the map, and there was no telling how many panic attacks it would take me to get there.

Well, folks, the itinerary arrived in my mailbox, and I was able to calculate approximately fourteen panic attacks in my future. One attack about every two hours of flying time. One way. And the same on the way home. But of course I wasn't exactly worried about coming home, because at this point I was fairly certain I'd die of a heart attack on the way there.

But as God would have it, I didn't return home in a casket. I returned home in an aircraft. And I emerged a shattered heart encased by a tired body.

I continue to return to Zimbabwe frequently without a single notion of slowing down. I freak out about the flights every time. But it is for Jesus, and for Jesus I will joyfully freak.

The first time I returned home from Zim, I recall enjoying my first thorough, hot shower in nearly seventeen days. The dirt on my feet just wouldn't wash off. Imagine the dust settling in. And then I realized it wasn't dirt. It was sun. The sun had permeated my skin and gone deep. I think it is possible that even my bones were suntanned. I observed strappy, tanned feet daily for many months after that and thought of it as a very special memento from my blessed time in Africa.

Then, one morning in the shower as I washed my feet, I realized the tan lines were gone. My feet looked disappointingly normal. They were unmarked. But hadn't I been there? Hadn't I served? Hadn't I been radically changed? There had been nothing attractive about my tanned feet. My sandals were sporty with many straps, which made for an interesting pattern. But when that pattern faded, it broke my heart. The precious memento I walked around with day to day was gone.

And then it resonated with me: Jesus wore sandals—sandals our feet will never be fit for. I bet His sweet feet were always dirty and dusty. He journeyed far. His beautiful feet did not stop walking to share the message of His love and the salvation offered through Him. The prophet Isaiah had spoken before Him and proclaimed, "How beautiful on the mountains are the feet of those who bring good news." That's a lot of worn-out feet.

Today I have fully and joyfully embarked on a blessed journey to love orphans to Christ and to help them survive in any way that Jesus provides. I have a zillion stories I could tell you about the children, about the ravages of AIDS, about the desperation of young African mothers placing their newborns in garbage piles. I could tell about a ten-year old boy who carried his seven-year-old sister to the hospital because nobody else would. And she died anyway.

I have stories and photographic images that might become a book someday, but for now I'd just like to share that going where Jesus sends you does not have to be met with trepidation and fear. He cares for you, and He knows what He is doing. He planned your footsteps far in advance of you ever deciding to go anywhere in His name. Whether you strap on your sandals and journey to the prison to offer ministry to incarcerated women, or you serve soup to the homeless at the local shelter, or you travel to nations where orphans out-populate the commoners, He has gone before you. Whatever happens to you, with you, and through you fits well within His divine plan. So go. In joy. In hope, walk with your beautiful feet in love. "And this is love: that we walk in obedience to his commands. As you have heard from the beginning, his command is that you walk in love" (2 John 6).

This much I know: We cannot walk in love if we are driven by guilt. We cannot walk in love if we are driven by fear. We cannot walk in love if we are living in shame. We cannot effectively serve Jesus and honor the gospel from those positions. Our service in the gospel commission needs to come from a burning desire in faith to honor His name. We have to authentically want to serve to increase the kingdom of heaven.

We can come to see that through His Spirit we have the capacity to participate in the salvation story. No, we cannot carry the sins of another, nor can we sacrifice our lives for the salvation of humanity. But Christ initiated the Great Commission. He "commissioned" His believers to do this work with Him and for Him. It is important work, and it requires sacrifice.

He didn't call for us to wait for such opportunities to bang down our doors and beg for our participation. If the opportunity shows up, that is fantastic. If the thing that stirs your heart to move doesn't come to you, go to it. Sometimes we just have to be willing to carve it out. Go to the well. Root deep. Overflow with thankfulness. Lean, stretch, turn around, and grow. Put someone's needs above your own. Lose sleep over the lost. Love Jesus every moment. This is life lived as joy being chosen. This is life on a journey to the kingdom. A life well watered.

There are a couple of significantly massive themes that run throughout all of Scripture, the collection of writings that we credit as being God's true Word. There is the good news message of salvation through Jesus on the cross. And then there is the message of destruction and punishment for those who refuse to accept the message of Christ. Heaven isn't significant only because of its promise to be eternal peace, but also because the only other alternative is eternal darkness and severe punishment.

Hell is reserved for unbelievers. "Good" people are destined for such darkness because of their unbelief. So my prayer is this: that if this book has offered anything to you, has offered you encouragement in knowing Jesus, loving Him, and treating this life as a journey to an eternal peace in heaven to be with Him, that you will speak the gospel in this broken world in hopes of protecting others from continuing on their way into darkness. Life, apparently, has two possible endings. I so desperately want for the end of our stories to be glory!

Heavenly Father, I feel at a loss for words to thank You for Your ever-flowing living waters, that with You we will never thirst. I praise Your precious name as I view the collection of us as Your well-watered garden, growing and blooming for Your glory. And Lord, as I sit here at the end of this written journey in an effort to glorify You, I am more aware than ever how full my buckets are, that You abundantly bless those who love You with unexplainable, unsearchable things, known only by the heart and mind and soul. You are our eternal treasure, O Lord. May we never fail to recognize that You are approachable, that You love us and want what is best for us according to Your plan, that You are nourishment to our spirits, and that in You we will never ever never thirst, because You have already given us eternal life. Sweet Lord, thank You for watering us so well. In Christ alone, amen.

A SPECIAL NOTE FROM THE AUTHOR

After my second trip to Zimbabwe, I founded a 501(c)3 Non-Profit charitable organization to serve as an orphan care ministry as well as a source for adoption grants. Please consider learning more about Beautiful Feet Global Outreach, Inc., and becoming a one-time donor, a monthly partner, or a child sponsor. Once our Zimbabwe initiatives are thriving, we will choose another orphanage in a different location to steward with love, hope, and resources.

www.BeautifulfeetGo.org

www.beautifulfeetgo.blogspot.com

www.BFGOmelissa.com

Twitter: @BFGOmelissa

www.facebook.com/BFGOorg

Made in the USA
Monee, IL
12 February 2021

60391055R00105